THE CHILD'S

HISTORY OF THE UNITED STATES.

DESIGNED AS A

FIRST BOOK OF HISTORY

FOR SCHOOLS.

ILLUSTRATED BY NUMEROUS ANECDOTES.

1831.

British Library Cataloguing-in-Publication Data
A catalogue record for this book is available from the
British Library

Charles A. Goodrich

Reverend Charles Augustus Goodrich was born in 1790. An American author and Congregational minister, he popularized the motto, 'a place for everything and everything in its place.' Goodrich attended Yale University in his youth, where he studied theology and graduated in 1812. Four years later, he became formally ordained and was appointed pastor of the First Congregational Church in Worcester, Massachusetts.

In 1820, Goodrich moved to Berlin, Connecticut, America, and in 1848 he moved again to Hartford, Connecticut. Goodrich continued to work as a pastor in Hartford and was also a member of the Connecticut Senate (the upper house of the Connecticut General Assembly, which had thirty six members, each representing a district with around 100,000 inhabitants). As well as this hefty workload, Goodrich also aided his brother, Samuel Goodrich (who published under the name of 'Peter Parley') in writing books for children. Charles Goodrich was the author of several books himself, passionate about the subjects of history, teaching the young and religion. He penned (among others): *View of Religions* (1829), *History of the United States of America* (1852-5), *Family Tourist* (1848), *Family Sabbath-Day Miscellany* (1855), *Geography of the Chief Places mentioned in the Bible* (1855), *Greek Grammar* (1855), and the *Child's History of the United States* (1855).

As has already been noted, Goodrich is also known for having the first printed citation of the epigram: 'Have a place for everything, and keep everything in its proper place.' The phrase was published in an article called 'Neatness' which Goodrich published in *The Ohio Repository* (Canton, Ohio), in December 1827. The idea that everything should have, and be kept in its place has subsequently appeared in many texts. In 1841 the phrase was used in a modified version in an item headed 'Brother Jonathan's Wife's Advice to her Daughter on her Marriage', in the *Hagerstown Mail*, Maryland: 'A place for everything and everything in time are good family mottos.' In *Masterman Ready, or the Wreck of the Pacific,* in 1842, Frederick Marryat wrote, 'In well-conducted man-of-war everything is in its place, and there is a place for everything.'

Charles Augustus Goodrich died on 4th June 1862, aged seventy-two.

PREFACE.

In presenting this little volume to the public, the author is not aware that he treads on ground at present occupied by any one. He indeed knows that several Histories of the United States for schools are in circulation; but they are obviously of a more elaborate character than the one here offered, and were designed for pupils of a more advanced standing. This is for *beginners*, and *only* for them.

The simplicity of the plan renders unnecessary any directions as to the manner in which the book is to be taught or studied.

Should any curiosity exist among *little folks* as to the author, he has only to say, at present, that he is not a *stranger* to them. He has laboured for their instruction and amusement; and nothing will delight him more than to learn that this little volume, on the history of their own country, contributes in any degree to make them useful and happy.

CONTENTS.

THE UNITED STATES.

FOR CHILDREN.

Columbus listening to the cry of "Land!" p. 4.

LESSON I.

AMERICA DISCOVERED BY COLUMBUS.

1. AMERICA was discovered in the year 1492, by *Christopher Columbus.* Columbus was born in Italy. He first went to sea when he was fourteen years of age. He was forty-five when he discovered America.

2. He sailed from a place in Spain, called *Palos*. Palos lies exactly east from Jamestown, in Virginia. Columbus came to America with three vessels. They were small vessels. They were called the *Santa Maria*, and *Pinta*, and the *Nigna*.

3. The ocean which Columbus crossed was the Atlantic. This is three thousand miles wide. No one had crossed this ocean before. He was two months in performing the voyage.

4. The land which he first saw was an island. He found it inhabited by Indians. The Indians called it *Gu-a-na-ha-na*. Columbus gave it the name of *San Salvador*. It is one of the West-India Islands called Bahamas. In the maps of the present day it is called *Cat Island*.

5. After this, Columbus made several other voyages. In 1498, he discovered the continent itself. Columbus died in 1506, when he was fifty-eight years old.

QUESTIONS.

1. When was America discovered? By whom? Where was Columbus born? At what age did he first go to sea? How old was he when he first discovered America?

2. What country did he sail from? From what place? Which way does Palos lie from Jamestown? How many vessels had Columbus? Were they large or small vessels? What were their names?

3. What ocean did Columbus cross? How wide is this ocean? Had any one crossed it before? How long did it take to perform the voyage?

4. What was the land which Columbus first saw? Who inhabited it? What did the Indians call the island? What name is given to it in the maps of the present day?

5. Did Columbus make other voyages? When did he discover the continent itself? In what year did he die? How old was he?

STORY.

1. Now that you know the first lesson, I will tell you a story. You have learned how Columbus discovered America. Before his time, the people in other countries knew not that there was any such land as America.

2. How, then, should Columbus *know* that there was any such land: he did *not* know. But he thought there might be; and he told his thoughts to some of the great men in Europe, but they paid little attention to him.

3. At length, he went into Spain, and the king and queen of that country treated him more kindly; and it was they who paid for the vessels in which Columbus sailed on his voyage of discovery.

4. This was a bold plan. No vessel had as yet crossed the wide Atlantic; but Columbus was brave, and his men were brave also.

5. For sixty days they sailed directly west, but they could not discover any land. And now the sailors became alarmed. They trembled to think of the distance they had sailed; and were fearful they might never return. The heart of Columbus alone remained firm. But he promised to return, if in three days land should not be discovered.

6. The evening of the third day came. It grew dark No land was in sight. Columbus walked the deck. He felt anxious. Presently, he heard a shout from on board the Pinta. What could it mean? A still louder shout he soon heard. The cry was "land! land!"

7. The heart of Columbus beat with joy, and the sailors wept for joy; and when the morning came, the land was in full view before them. Columbus assembled his men around him, and with them returned thanks to God; and then they sung a hymn of praise.

8. After this Columbus landed on the island. The inhabitants were Indians; they had never seen a white man before; they were surprised to see Columbus, but they were astonished at the sight of his vessels, and at the fire and thunder of the cannon.

9. When Columbus had sufficiently examined the country, he set sail to return. But a storm came on, and the waves of the ocean rose like mountains. The masts trembled; the sails were torn; and all was given up for lost.

10. The little vessels, however, struggled through the waves. They mounted aloft where they stood, for a moment—then they plunged—and then again they arose. At length, the tempest ceased. God had preserved them. And now they went on their way; and after sailing for many days and weeks, they arrived safely in Spain, and there they told of the *new world* which they had discovered.

Capt. Smith on an Island. p. 10.

LESSON II.

JAMESTOWN SETTLED BY THE ENGLISH.

1. AMERICA was now discovered, and the news spread far and wide. Vessels were fitted out, and many daring men came to make further discoveries. One who came was called *A-mer-i-cus Ves-pu-cius.* He did not discover much, but he told *so fine a story*, that America was called after him. It should have been called after Columbus.

2. Another who came was *John Cabot*. He sailed from England. He discovered North-America in which we live. This was in 1497.

3. Many years after this, some people from England came over to settle in America. They consisted of one hundred and five persons. They were four months on the water, and their voyage was very unpleasant.

4. On reaching America they entered Chesapeake Bay, and sailing up James River about thirty-two miles, they found a beautiful spot on its banks, where they concluded to settle. This they called *Jamestown*.

5. The country then was all a wilderness. There were no houses, nor roads, nor bridges, as at the present day; and the only houses which the English had to live in for a long time, were built of logs.

6. For a time, they had plenty of provisions, which they brought with them. But when

these were gone, they suffered much, and were often near starving. Then they were obliged to live on fish, and acorns, and roots, and a little corn, which the Indians gave them.

7. Their sufferings were often great. Sometimes they were in want. Sometimes many were sick, and many died. And then, again, the Indians threatened to kill them. But, after a time, other vessels came from England, and brought more people, and supplies of food.

QUESTIONS.

1. After whom was America called? After whom should it have been called?

2. Who discovered North-America? When did Cabot discover it?

3. What people first settled in America? How many came over? How long was their voyage? Was the voyage pleasant?

4. What bay did they enter? What river did they enter? How far did they sail up that river? Where did they settle? What did they call the place?

5. What was the appearance of the country? What kind of houses did they live in?

6. On what, at first, did they live? When their provisions were gone, what did they do?

7. Did they suffer much? From what did they suffer? How were they relieved?

STORY.

1. Now I will tell you another story. You have learned how many years after America was discovered, some people from England came over to settle in the country. Among those who came in the first vessel, was *Captain John Smith;* and it is about his adventures I am going to tell you.

2. Captain Smith was born in England. When quite young, he lost his father; and having no one to take care of him but his mother, he became wild and disobedient.

3. After a time, he was placed with a merchant, by whom he was treated kindly. But his conduct was very improper; and at length he ran away.

4. He had but little money with him. With this money he travelled towards France. He had heard of Paris, a beautiful city of France, and he wished to see it.

5. At length, he reached that city, and admired it much. The houses, which he saw, were very high and beautiful; but he was better pleased with the shows, of which the French people are very fond. In one place, he saw some wild animals, lions, tigers, elephants, and monkeys. In another place, he saw a man dancing on a rope; and not far distant, people riding very swiftly in a place called a *circus.* One man was standing upright on

a horse, under full gallop; and another with one foot on one horse, and the other foot on another horse.

6. When Smith had seen enough of France, he went to Holland, where the Dutch live. Here he became a soldier; but not liking this kind of life, one dark night he deserted. It was well that he escaped. Had he been taken, he would have been shot; and here, then, we should have ended our story.

7. After this he made a voyage to Italy. On board the vessel in which he sailed, there were several passengers besides himself. One day young Smith treated some of these quite rudely; upon which, they threw him overboard into the sea. He sunk deep; but being a good swimmer, he was soon on the top of the waves, and at length reached an island, from which he was taken by some people belonging to another vessel, and carried to Italy.

8. When he had seen Italy, he went into Austria, where he again enlisted as a soldier, and went forth to fight the Turks. One day, a Turkish horseman sent a challenge to him to come and fight. Smith and the Turk fought on horseback, and with a kind of sword, called a *sabre*. Smith killed the Turk; and after him two others.

9. After this, in a battle, he was taken prisoner and sold as a slave, and was carried many hundred miles far to the

east. Here he was loaded with chains, and now became very miserable. No wonder he *was* miserable. Persons who conduct themselves so improperly as he did, must expect to suffer. God approves not of wicked conduct ; nor will he bless those who are guilty of it.

10. After a long time, Captain Smith made his escape, and returned to England. He had seen much, and suffered more. His misfortunes had done him good ; and after this he proved a useful man.

11. Soon after his return to England, he was invited to accompany the first settlers to America. This invitation he accepted, and accordingly came over, assisted in building Jamestown, and in America proved very useful.

13. I have something further to relate about Captain Smith. This I shall do in my next story. But, before reading that story, be careful to learn the next lesson. When *I* was a boy, it used to be told me, "work first—then play." In like manner I would say, to all my little pupils, "learn the lesson first—then read the story."

Pocahantas saving the life of Capt. Smith. p. 17.

LESSON III.

INDIANS.

1. Soon after the English had come to America, they found that the whole land was filled with Indians. Their number was about one hundred and fifty thousand, in the present limits of the United States.

2. How long the Indians had been in America is not known. It is supposed they came

from Asia, across Bhering's Strait. This strait separates America from Asia.

3. The Indians were quite tall, and very straight; their colour was red, or brown. They had long, black, and coarse hair. They were very brave, but cruel and revengeful.

4. Their huts they called *week-wams*. They lived on the flesh of wild animals and fish. Sometimes they had corn, beans, peas, and potatoes. The English never saw Indian corn, before they came to America. It is called *Indian* corn, because it was found among the Indians. Their name for it was *maize*.

5. The Indians in America were divided into *tribes*. Each tribe had a king, or chief, whòm they called their *sachem*. Between these tribes there were often bloody wars. Indians delight in war. The weapons which they used were clubs, bows and arrows, and tomahawks.

6. The tomahawk was made of stone, and

with it they used to cut off the top part of the heads of those they took prisoners. This was called *scalping*. Before going out to war, they always sounded the war-hoop. This was a yell, sounding like, "*Wo-ach, Wo-ach, ha hach Wo-ach!*" When they made peace, each smoked the same pipe. This pipe was called a *Calumet*. It was made of red stone. Its stem was more than a yard long. It was ornamented with porcupine's quills, beads, ribbons, and horse-hair dyed red. The Indians worshipped a Good Spirit and an Evil Spirit. But of the true God they knew nothing; nor had they ever heard of the Bible, or of Jesus Christ the Saviour of men.

QUESTIONS.

1. Who inhabited America before the English came over? What was the number of Indians in the bounds of the United States?

2. How long had they lived in America? From what country did they come? Across what strait? What does this strait separate?

3. What was the appearance of the Indians? What was their colour? What kind of hair had they? Were they brave? Were they kind and forgiving?

4. What were their huts called? On what did they live? On what else? Was Indian corn known to the English before they came to America? Why was it called *Indian* corn? What did the Indians call it?

5. How were the Indians divided? What was their chief called? What is said of wars between them? In what do Indians delight? What are their weapons of war?

6. Of what was the tomahawk made? What was its use? What is scalping? What did the Indians do before going to war? What did the war-hoop sound like? When peace was made, what did they do? What was this pipe called?

7. What did the Indians worship? What did they know of the true God? What of the Bible, and Jesus Christ?

STORY.

1. I will now finish my story about Captain Smith.

2. The Indians, at first, seemed well pleased to see Captain Smith, and the other English people. For a time, they treated them kindly, and gave them corn.

3. But their kindness did not last long. They began to think the English wished to get away all their lands And, at length, they did not come to Jamestown often; nor would they give the new settlers any more corn, nor sell them any.

4. The English were now in want; and many feared that they must all starve. But Captain Smith being a brave man, went boldly among the Indians, and compelled them to let him have corn.

5. But this made them unfriendly to him, and now they watched an opportunity to seize him. And not long after, they did seize him. He had gone into the wilderness, some distance from Jamestown, when some Indians came upon him, and took him, though he bravely defended himself for a long time.

6. The Indians were much pleased, that they had him in their power. They shouted over him, and around him; and, at length, bound him to a tree, thinking to kill him with their arrows.

7. Some said, however, that it was best to take him to *Po-ha-tan*. He was their sachem, and a mighty warrior. This was agreed upon, and they led Captain Smith to Pohatan.

8. When Pohatan saw him, he seemed well pleased. He had, he thought, an enemy in his power. Indians delight in torture and blood; and now Pohatan and his warriors said Captain Smith should die.

9. Preparations were made. A stone was brought and laid on the ground. The Indians gathered round. They looked fierce, and were impatient for his death. Captain Smith's head was laid on the stone, and a club was handed to Pohatan.

10. Pohatan came forward, and stood over where Captain Smith lay. Near by stood two little girls. They

were the daughters of Pohatan. The name of the one I do not know—the name of the other was *Poc-a-han-tas.*

11. These little girls saw Captain Smith—they saw their father—they saw the club. The strong arm of the chief was raising it. He looked full of wrath, and death was coming in the blow.

12. But the blow came not—and death came not. Both *were* coming—but little Pocahantas, at that instant, sprang forward and folded the head of Captain Smith in her arms. She could not see him die. He was a brave man, and she wished her father not to kill a brave man.

13. Pohatan paused. He looked round amazed. The fierce and savage looks of the Indians were gone. They loved Pocahantas, and she *was* a lovely girl. Pohatan himself was much affected. He raised his daughter. No doubt he loved her better than ever. For *her* sake, he spared Captain Smith, and sent him back to Jamestown in safety.

14. This was noble. Pocahantas had been brought up among savages; but she had kind feelings, and in this instance, set a worthy example.

Goodman and Brown discovering Plymouth at sunrise. p. 23.

LESSON IV.

PLYMOUTH SETTLED.

1. SEVEN years after the English had settled at Jamestown, some Dutch people came over from Holland, and began to settle *New-York*. They built a fort at *Albany*, and formed a settlement where the city of *New-York* now stands. The year the Dutch came over was 1614.

2. In 1620, another vessel came from England, bringing people who began to settle *Massachusetts*. On board this vessel, there were an hundred and one persons. The name of the vessel in which they came was the *Speedwell*.

3. These persons were a *religious* set of people. They were called *Puritans*; and this name was given them, because they wished to worship God in a *purer* manner than other people did in England. But this they were not allowed to do in peace, and so they concluded to come to America.

4. Their voyage lasted four months, and was very distressing. They settled in a place which they called *Plymouth*. This lies thirty-six miles south-east from Boston. They landed on the twenty-second of December. They landed on a rock, which since that time has been called "*Forefathers' Rock*." The first

person who jumped out of the boat on to the rock, was a girl, by the name of *Mary Chilton*.

5. When they landed, the ground was covered with a deep snow; and they suffered much before they could finish a sufficient number of log houses. They suffered also from hunger; but the Indians round Plymouth were quite friendly, and gave them corn. But before spring, more than half of the people died.

6. Not long after this, several other vessels arrived with people, who settled Boston, Salem, and other places.

QUESTIONS.

1. Who settled New-York? How long was the arrival of the Dutch after the English began to settle Jamestown? Where did the Dutch build a fort? Where did the Dutch form a settlement? What year was this?

2. When was Massachusetts first settled? By whom? How many first came over? What was the name of the vessel, in which they came over?

3. What sort of people were they? What were they called? Why were they called thus? Were they allowed to do this in peace?

4. How long was their voyage? Was it pleasant? Where did they settle? How far is this from Boston? Which way? When did they land? On what did they land? What is this rock called? Who first jumped from the boat?

5. What was the ground covered with at this time? Did the people suffer much? From what did they suffer? Who gave them corn? How many died before spring?

6. What other places were settled soon after this?

STORY.

1. You now know something of the arrival of the people at Plymouth, in America, and of their landing on "Forefathers' Rock."

2. It was winter when they arrived, as I told you; but they contrived to build nineteen huts, one for each family. But all the time they were at work, the cold wind blew, and it rained, and snowed. Many of the men took cold, fell sick, and died.

3. The people, however, prayed much, and still trusted in God. They had come to America to serve HIM; and they believed that He would not forsake them. And He did not forsake them. They suffered much from sickness, and from want, and many died. But spring, at length, came; and those who lived enjoyed better health, and were able to work.

4. One day in the month of January, John Goodman and Peter Brown went into the woods to get some thatch, or wild grass, with which to cover their houses. They had no shingles and no straw, but used wild grass.

5. When they had procured some, they set out to return; but these men had lost their way, and before they were aware, night came on; the sky was cloudy, and it began to snow. What should they do? They had no great coats, and their clothes were thin.

6. They could not reach home that night. Fortunately, they found a rock, under which they took shelter, and on some leaves they laid down, and with other leaves they covered themselves.

7. But now another trouble came. John Goodman said he was sure that he heard a lion near them. Peter Brown listened, and thought he heard one too. They were much alarmed, and lay as still as possible.

8. I suppose my pupils know, that they did *not* hear a lion. Lions were never found in North-America. Some very good people used to say that there certainly *was* a lion once seen at Cape Ann, near Boston; but wiser people know that there never were any seen there. Lions are found in Africa; but not in America, unless they are brought here for a show.

9. Now I will tell you what Peter Brown and John Goodman *did* hear. What they heard was nothing but the roaring of the wind: but they thought it was the roaring of a lion; and they were so sure of it, that they both

rose and began climbing a tree: but they were soon glad to come down, the wind was so strong and cold.

10. When they reached the ground, they were obliged to walk round and round the tree to keep themselves from freezing, and they continued to walk all night. It was well that they were kept awake by the fear of a lion. Had they gone to sleep under the rock, they would have been frozen to death.

11. No lion came near them, for no lion was there. The morning at length dawned, and glad were they. They now hastened from the spot; and at length came to a hill, from the top of which they could see Plymouth harbour. It was a great distance; and fast were they obliged to walk, and sometimes even to run, to reach home that night. At nine in the evening they entered the village.

12. The people were rejoiced to see them. They had been abroad all that day in search of them, but they could not find them; and it was the general opinion, that they had been killed by the Indians. I dare say that John Goodman and Peter Brown took good care not to get lost again.

John Holmes passing the Dutch Fort. p. 29.

LESSON V.

OTHER SETTLEMENTS.

1. Now you know something of the manner in which Virginia, New-York, and Massachusetts, began to be settled. You will wish to know, I trust, when and how some other of the United States began to be settled. I will tell you.

2. *New-Hampshire* was settled next to Mas-

sachusetts, by people who came from England. They settled at a place called *Dover*, on the river Pis-cat-a-qua. This was in 1623.

3. *New-Jersey* was settled next—in 1624. This was settled by people from Norway. The town they settled was called *Bergen*, after a city of that name in Norway. It lies on the Hudson, three miles from the city of New-York.

4. Next to New-Jersey, *Delaware* was settled: this was in 1627. The people who settled this state came from Sweden and Finland. They settled near *Wilmington*.

5. The state of *Connecticut* was settled next—in 1633; that is, the first house was at that time erected. This was a trading house, built by one *John Holmes*, at Windsor, seven or eight miles north of Hartford, on Connecticut River. In 1635, and the following year, the three towns, Hartford, Windsor, and Wethersfield,

were all settled, by people from Massachusetts, who travelled on foot through the wilderness. They were a fortnight in making the journey. The distance is a hundred miles. They lived chiefly on the milk of the cows which they drove.

6. *Maryland* was settled in 1634, by persons who came from England with Lord Baltimore.

7. *Rhode-Island* was settled in 1636, by Roger Williams and some others, from Massachusetts. They settled the town of *Providence.*

8. *Georgia* was settled in 1733, by people from England, who were brought over by General Oglethorpe. They settled at *Savannah.*

9. The first settlement made in *North-Carolina* was in the year 1650, by people from Virginia.

10. *South-Carolina* was settled in 1670, near the city of *Charleston.*

11. *Pennsylvania* was first settled in 1681.

It was called after William Penn, who was a Quaker. He founded the city of *Philadelphia*. This word means the *city of love*.

12. Thus I have told you about the settlement of *thirteen* states. There are now twenty-four states; but only thirteen were settled before the war of the Revolution, about which I shall tell you by and by.

13. Now remember the order in which these thirteen states were settled. First, Virginia; next, New-York; then, Massachusetts; New-Hampshire; New-Jersey; Delaware; Connecticut; Maryland; Rhode-Island; North-Carolina; South-Carolina; Pennsylvania; and last, Georgia.

QUESTIONS.

2. What state was settled next to Massachusetts? By whom? What place did they settle? On what river? In what year?
3. What state was next settled? In what year? By whom? What town did they settle? How far is this town from New-York? On what river?
4. When was Delaware settled? By whom? Near what place did they settle?

5. When was Connecticut settled? What house was at this time erected? By whom? Where? How far from Hartford? Which way? On what river? When were Hartford, Windsor, and Weathersfield, settled? By whom? How did they reach these places? How long did it take them? What is the distance? On what did they live?

6. When was Maryland settled? By whom?

7. When was Georgia settled? By whom? Who brought them over? Where did they settle?

8. When was Rhode-Island settled? By whom? What town did they settle?

9. When was North-Carolina settled? By whom?

10. When was South-Carolina settled? Near what city?

11. When was Pennsylvania settled? After whom was it called? What was he? What city did he found?

12. How many states have I told you about? How many states are there now in the United States? How many states were there settled before the Revolutionary War?

13. Now, in what order were these states settled?

STORY.

1. Children of the present day know little of the toil and trouble it cost our fathers and mothers to settle these states. Now, we can look abroad and see large cities, handsome villages, fine fields, and rich gardens. We see good, smooth roads, strong bridges, and well finished houses.

2. It was not so once. Indeed, it was not. When these states were first settled, the country was all a wilderness. For hundreds of miles it was one unbroken forest. Not a city, not a town was to be seen—not a village—not

a house, excepting here and there a few Indian week-wams.

3. Even the frame of the first house ever built in Connecticut, was made at Plymouth, in Massachusetts. It was there made by one John Holmes. And when he had finished it, he put it on board a small vessel, and set sail for Connecticut River.

4. Up that river he went; and, at length, came where Hartford now stands. Just in that spot, he was much surprised to see a kind of fort, standing near the banks of the river. Some Dutch people from New-York had built it, and they were at this time in the fort; and they were determined that no other people should settle near them; and they had planted a cannon to fire upon any one, who should dare to sail up the river.

5. When Holmes came along in his vessel, out came the Dutch, from the fort, and hailed him. "Stop," said they "pull down your sails;" and while they said this, they loaded their cannon, and brought fire from the fort, and told Holmes, that they would blow him through if he did not stop.

6. Holmes saw the Dutch, saw their cannon, saw them loading it, and heard them call. Little cared he; he was a bold man. A fine wind was blowing, and his little

vessel went on, like a bird in the air. Besides, he knew that the Dutch were no marksmen at all; and he went on, leaving them quite vexed that powder and ball would not scare an Englishman. On he went, I said—reached Windsor—put up his house, and thus led the way for the settlement of Connecticut.

Canonchet replying to the young English officer. p. 37.

LESSON VI.

EARLY INDIAN WARS.—1. PEQUOT WAR.

1. I HAVE already told you something about the Indians, who were found in the country, when it was first settled by the English. In this lesson, I shall tell you of the *wars*, which the English had with these Indians.

2. The *first* Indian war was called the "*Pequot* war." This began in 1637.

3. The Pequots were a powerful tribe. They lived in Connecticut. Their chief sachem was called *Sassacus*. He was a great warrior.

4. The Pequots had two forts near New-London and Groton. Soon after the English settled Connecticut, the Pequots killed several of them, and a war with them became necessary.

5. The people of Hartford, Windsor, and Wethersfield, raised ninety men. Captain Mason commanded them. They were assisted by five hundred Narragansett Indians. These Indians lived in Rhode-Island.

6. With this force, Captain Mason surprised the principal fort of the Pequots early one morning—burnt the fort, and utterly destroyed them. This was a sad war; but it was just on the part of the English, because the Pequots were determined to destroy them.

2. PHILIP'S WAR.

7. The *next* Indian war began in 1675. This was called "*King Philip's war*," because he was the chief mover of it.

8. Philip was the sachem of the *Wam-pa-no-ag* tribe. He had a fort at Mount Hope, in Bristol, Rhode-Island.

9. The grandfather of Philip was the friend of the English. Philip was their enemy. He was their enemy, because he thought they were taking too much land from the Indians; and now he determined, if possible, to destroy them.

10. To effect this purpose, he visited almost all the tribes in New-England, and engaged them to help him on in the war. The war was now begun. It was a more extensive war than the Pequot war. It was more bloody.

11. Many towns were surprised, and the inhabitants cruelly killed. At Brookfield, in Massachusetts, the inhabitants fled to a house,

and the Indians came up, and fired at it, and continued round it for two days. And, at length, they loaded a cart with flax and tow, and setting it on fire, pushed it against the house. But a heavy shower of rain came, and put out the fire.

12. At another time, the English troops followed the Narragansett Indians, who had taken part with Philip, into a deep swamp, in which they had a fort and a village of weekwams. In the fort and village were supposed to be nearly four thousand Indians. The English attacked the fort, and a dreadful battle followed; but the English were victorious. They burnt the fort and the weekwams, and almost all the Indians were killed or burnt.

13. The war ended in 1676, by the death of Philip. He was discovered at this time in a swamp, with his great captain *Anawou*, and a few followers. Capt. Church being informed

of it, marched to the swamp, and ordered his soldiers to surround it.

14. "Now," said he, "it is impossible for Philip to escape." At this moment, Philip started to flee. An English soldier levelled his gun at him, but it missed fire. An Indian fired, and the ball passed through his heart.

15. Captain Church ordered him to be beheaded. This service was performed by an Indian, who, as he stood over Philip, said: "You have been one very great man. You have made many a man afraid of you. But so big as you be, I will chop you to pieces."

QUESTIONS.

2. What was the first Indian war called? When did it begin?
3. What is said of the Pequot tribe? Where did they live? Who was their chief sachem? What is said of him?
4. What two forts had the Pequots? How did they treat the English?
5. How many men did the English raise for the war? By what towns were they raised? Who commanded them? By whom were they assisted? Where did the Narragansetts live?
6. What was the fate of the Pequots? Was this war just on the part of the English? Why?
7. When did the next Indian war begin? What was this war called? Why? Of what tribe was Philip the sachem? Where was his fort?

9. What is said of the grandfather of Philip? What is said of Philip himself? Why was Philip an enemy to the English? What did he determine to do?

10. To effect his purpose, what did he do? How did this war compare with the Pequot war?

11. What were surprised? Who were killed? What did the inhabitants at Brookfield do? How long did the Indians surround this house? In what way did they attempt to set fire to the house?

12. At another time, where did the English troops follow the Indians? What tribe was this? In the fort and village, how many Indians were there supposed to be? What became of the fort, week-wams, and Indians?

13. When did the war end? What was the occasion? Where was Philip discovered? Who was with him? What did Capt. Church order his soldiers to do?

14. Who attempted to shoot Philip as he fled? Why did he fail? Who did kill him?

15. What was done with Philip? Who beheaded him? What did the Indian say?

STORY.

1. My story, at this time, will be about *Ca-non-chet* and *Philip*.

2. *Canonchet* was the friend of Philip. He was the sachem of the Narragansetts, a tribe which I told you lived in Rhode-Island. Canonchet was a proud chief, and a bold warrior.

3. After the swamp fight, of which I have told you, some English troops came upon him. He fled before them, and plunged himself into a river. But his foot slip-

ped, and he fell so deep, that he was taken as he rose; and after he was taken, he said that he was now only like "a rotten stick."

4. But his appearance was still noble. His eye was black; and keenly was it fixed upon the English. They were struck with the majesty of his looks. A young English soldier asked him a question. The proud warrior replied, "You are a child: I answer no question of yours. Let your chief come, I will answer him."

5. Canonchet was doomed to die. "Well," said he, "I wish to die—I wish to die before I have spoken any thing unworthy of *Canonchet.*"

6. *Philip* was as proud as Canonchet, and a still greater man. He was a warrior of a lofty spirit—bold and powerful; and at the same time, artful and treacherous.

7. To the English, after the war began, his name was a constant terror. Wherever he passed, he spread dismay around him—he asked no favour for himself or followers, and shewed none to his enemies.

8. After all, let not Philip be too severely condemned. He was a savage, and lived in savage times. He had had no religious instruction—no, he was a heathen—an unenlightened heathen, who sought glory in war and revenge for injuries.

9. Philip had *some* reason, too, to think that the English

were his enemies. He was a king, and had a just claim to the country. He *thought* the English wished to drive him and his followers away, and get their lands for nothing. In this he mistook. But, perhaps, the English were not sufficiently cautious, not to excite his suspicions.

10. If such were his belief, is it strange that he was roused? Who would not fight for country, for wife, and children? For these he fought, fought like a hero, fought like a patriot, and we may add, fought like a savage!

11. It was sad, indeed, that Philip was so jealous of the English. A more dreadful war was never known in America, than Philip's war. Yet the blood shed in it might have been saved, had he only been convinced that the English were his friends.

Meeting of Mrs. Dustan and family. p. 43.

LESSON VII.

KING WILLIAM'S WAR.

1. PHILIP's war ended, as I told you, in 1676. The English people in America had now a period of rest. But this did not last long. Another war came. It was called "*King William's war.*" It began in 1690.

2. William was king of England. Louis XIV. was king of France. Louis declared war against William.

3. The people who had settled in that part of America, now called the United States, were subjects of King William. The people in Canada had come from France, and were subjects of King Louis.

4. When Louis had declared war against William, he sent orders to his people in Canada to make war upon the English people, who had settled in Massachusetts, Connecticut, and other places.

5. This war lasted seven years. Many Indians fought with the French, against the English. They frequently came down from Canada, sometimes in the midst of winter; they surprised towns in the dead of night, killed the inhabitants, and burnt their houses.

9. One winter in February, a party of French and Indians came to *Schenectady*. This place lies sixteen miles west of Albany. They came in the dead of night. It was a cold and pierc-

ing night. The snow was deep, and still it was snowing fast. The people were all asleep. The place was burnt—sixty of the inhabitants were slain; and many who escaped, were frozen to death.

7. The war ended in 1697.

QUESTIONS.

1. When did the Pequot war end? What is said of the state of the English people after this? Did peace last long? What was the war called which now came on? What year did it begin?

2. Who was William? Who was Louis XIV.? Against whom did Louis declare war?

3. What people in America were subjects of King William? What people were subjects of King Louis?

4. After war was declared, what order did Louis send to his people in Canada?

5. How long did this war last? Who fought with the French? When did they come down from Canada? What did they do?

6. What place did they attack in February? Which way is Schenectady from Albany? How many miles? Was it a clear or a stormy night? Were the inhabitants asleep or awake? What became of the place? How many of the people were killed? What befel many others?

7. When did the war end?

STORY.

1. King William's war ended in 1697. In the winter of that year, a sad event took place, and to that my story relates.

2. There lived at Haverhill, in New-Hampshire, a *Mr. Dustan.* He had a wife and eight children. They were all small. One was a little babe only a week old, and Mrs. Dustan was still sick.

3. One day, Mr. Dustan was in the field at work, when he saw a party of Indians crossing the field towards his house. He mounted his horse and reached the house, took his little children and put them in the road, and told them to run, and he would soon follow.

4. By this time the Indians had arrived. He was obliged to leave Mrs. Dustan and the babe, and on his horse he fled. He soon came up with his little children, though they run as fast as they could. He looked back, and some of the Indians were coming. What should he do?

5. For a moment he thought that he would take up the little boy or girl that he loved best, and flee. But which should he choose? He loved them all; and he could not choose. He told them to run fast, and he would try to stop the Indians.

6. He stopped his horse, and the children fled. He loaded his gun. The Indians soon came up. He fired, and again he fled. The Indians fired, but the balls touched him not, and touched not the children. God preserved them.

7. Again Mr. Dustan halted, and again loaded his gun;

and when the Indians came up he fired, and they fired also. But the same kind Providence protected him; and, at length, he and all his little children safely reached a house, and the Indians went back.

8. I wish I could add that Mrs. Dustan and her little babe were as safe. But it was not so. The babe was killed, and its poor mother, though sick, the savages compelled to travel, weak as she was, one hundred and fifty miles.

9. She now expected to be killed. But one night while the Indians were asleep, she made her escape, with two other prisoners. A long and dreary wilderness was before them, which they traversed with much toil; but at length they reached Haverhill. She found that her house was burned, but her husband was spared, and her seven little children.

10. The meeting between the mother and the children I shall not attempt to describe. I dare say that they flocked about her; and I dare say, too, that each one imprinted a kiss upon her cheek, and each was kissed many a time in return.

11. How thankful should children at the present day be, that there are no Indians to injure them, either by night or by day. It is God who causes them to see better days, and HIM they should love and serve

Massacre and burning at Deerfield, by the Indians. p. 46.

LESSON VIII.

QUEEN ANNE'S WAR.

1. QUEEN Anne ascended the throne of England in 1702. That year, war was again declared between France and England. It was called "*Queen Anne's war.*" And now again the French in Canada, and the English colonies in America, were engaged against each other.

2. The Indians in Canada assisted the French, and with them often came down upon the English, as they had done during King William's war. Several towns were burned, and much alarm and distress were caused.

3. The colonies which suffered most during this war, were those of Massachusetts and New-Hampshire.

4. This war ended in 1713. It had lasted eleven years: but like most other wars, little good was done by it.

QUESTIONS.

1. When did Queen Anne ascend the throne of England? In what year was war declared between France and England? What was this war called? What people in America were now engaged against each other?

2. Who assisted the French in this war? In what manner did the French and Indians treat the English?

5. Which colonies suffered the most?

4. When did the war end? How long had it lasted? What good had it brought to pass?

STORY.

1. My story must again be a sad one.

2. In the winter of 1704, three hundred French and

Indians came into Deerfield, in Massachusetts. It was in the dead of night. The inhabitants were asleep. Some persons had been set to keep watch; but even they were asleep.

3. At length, the Indians and French came to the house of Mr. Williams. He was the minister of Deerfield. They broke open his door—seized him—bound him—and kept him standing in the cold an hour, without his clothes.

4. Then they killed two of his children, and a servant of his family. Other savages had set fire to the town, and the flames were now rolling upward from every quarter. But one house was left standing, and in that the marks of the bullet are seen at the present day.

5. Forty-seven persons were killed, and one hundred taken into captivity. Among these latter were Mr. Williams and his family. The next day, Mrs. Williams was killed, in sight of her husband, and seventeen others were killed before they reached Canada.

6. Mr. Williams was kept a prisoner two years. At the end of this time, he was permitted to return to Deerfield, with fifty-seven of his people. After this, he preached for twelve years; and at length, went to his grave in peace.

View of Quebec. p. 51.

LESSON IX.

FRENCH AND INDIAN WAR.

1. QUEEN Anne's war, I said, ended in 1713. From this date, we shall pass rapidly on to the year 1756. In this latter year, the "*French and Indian*" war began.

2. Between these two wars, was a period of forty-two years, and during this time the English colonies in America flourished. The

inhabitants increased; agriculture was improved; commerce was extended; but manufactures did not flourish. The people in England were unwilling that the Americans should manufacture cloth, or hats, and scarcely anything else; because they wished the Americans to purchase of them. Still, the colonies flourished. In 1756, the thirteen colonies contained more than a million of inhabitants.

3. This year, the French and Indian war began. On the other side of the Atlantic, the war was carried on between England and France. In America, it was carried on between the English colonies, and the French and Indians in Canada.

4. This was an important war. In former wars, the English colonies had found it enough to defend their own territory. In this war, they sent troops to Canada to attack the French there. The English troops amounted to eight

thousand. They were commanded by General Wolfe.

5. The French troops were commanded by General Montcalm. Sept. 13th, 1759, the two armies met near Quebec. A bloody battle ensued. General Wolfe was killed. General Montcalm was wounded, in consequence of which he died. The English were victorious. The city of Quebec fell into the hands of the English.

6. This led the way to further success. All Canada was conquered; and, since that time, has been owned by the King of England. The war ended in 1763. It had lasted nearly seven years.

7. During this war the English colonists proved themselves to be a brave people. They spent much money, and at the close of the war they felt themselves poor. They were not well treated by England. It was, after all, *her*

war, and she ought to have paid them back the money which they had spent: but she would not do it, and they could not help themselves, because they had no power to compel her to do them justice.

QUESTIONS.

1. When did Queen Anne's war end? When did the French and Indian war begin?

2. How long was it between these two wars? What was the state of the English colonies during this period? What is said of their increase? What of agriculture? What of commerce? What of manufactures? Why were the people of England unwilling that the Americans should manufacture for themselves? How many inhabitants did the colonies contain in 1756?

3. When did the war begin? Between whom was the war carried on on the other side of the Atlantic? In America, between whom?

4. In former wars, what had the English colonies found it enough for themselves to do? In this war, where did they send troops? What number? Who commanded them?

5. Who commanded the French troops? When did the two armies meet? Near what place? What ensued? Who was killed? Who was wounded? What became of General Montcalm? Who were victorious? What city was taken? By whom?

6. To what did this lead the way? What country was conquered? By whom has it been since owned? When did this war end? How long had it lasted?

7. During this war, what did the English colonies prove themselves to be? What did they spend? What is said of them at the close of the war? Were they well treated by England? What ought she to have done? Did she pay them? Why could not they help themselves?

STORY.

1. The capture of Quebec, my pupils should know, was an *important* and *wonderful* event.

2. I will first tell them why it was important. It was so, because it may be said to have put an end to the war. The whole of Canada soon fell into the power of the English.

3. It was important, too, because it put an end to a long course of bloody wars. The English colonies had suffered greatly from the French and Indians during the wars of King William and Queen Anne, and now during the French and Indian war. But they had no more to fear, now that Canada belonged to the English.

4. The capture of Quebec was also a very wonderful event, because it was thought impossible to take it. And I think you will say that General Wolfe and his troops were bold and brave men to have attempted it.

5. At the beginning of the lesson is a view of Quebec, as you would see it were you sailing towards it down the river St. Lawrence. Look back at the picture, and I will explain how the city was taken by the English.

6. You see by the picture, that the upper part of Quebec is built on a high bank. From the level of the water

to the highest point, it is three hundred and forty-five feet. General Wolfe well knew that he could not capture the place, unless he could succeed in reaching these heights.

7. On the twelfth of September—this was in the year 1759—one hour after midnight, he put his troops on board some boats, and directed his course to a cove, or small bay, into which you see a vessel is entering. The boats entered this cove, which is now called "Wolfe's Cove;" and here, under the precipice, they landed, a mile and a half above the city.

8. Even here the precipice was nearly two hundred feet high, and quite steep. Yet steep and rugged as it was, Wolfe led his army up, and formed them on the plains above, within sight of the city. These plains are called the "*plains of Abraham.*" The towers which you see have been built since that time, and are called the "*Martello towers.*"

9. Here, on this plain, the army of Wolfe and the army of Montcalm met. They were nearly equal in numbers, and together amounted to ten thousand men.

10. The battle was desperate and bloody. Early in the action, General Wolfe was wounded in the wrist, and soon after another bullet entered near his thigh, and a third followed which pierced his breast. He sunk upon the

shoulder of a soldier, and was soon in the agonies of death. At this moment, the shout of "They fly! they fly!" was heard. For a moment he raised himself, and eagerly asked, "Who fly?" and being told it was the French, he said, "I die contented!"

11. The battle now went on. The French fled, and were slaughtered by hundreds with the bayonet and broad-sword. The brave Montcalm was mortally wounded; and the arms of the English were completely victorious.

The inhabitants of Boston hanging the Tory image. p. 58.

LESSON X.

WAR OF THE REVOLUTION.—STAMP ACT.

1. The "*War of the Revolution*" began in 1775. It is so called, because it ended in the *Independence of America.*

2. Until this time, the colonies in America were subject to the King of England. The country was settled by his subjects, and it was considered right, therefore, that he should govern it.

3. This the colonists were willing he should do, so long as his laws were just and good. They had come from England, and they loved the English people, and they respected the King, who was then George III.

4. But neither the King, nor the people in England, loved the Americans as much. They were always jealous of them. They feared that at some future time the Americans would become rich and powerful, and wish to separate from them.

5. The Americans were, indeed, prospering. They now amounted to more than three millions of people. The great men in England said, they were growing too fast—they would soon become proud and independent. Something must be done to keep them in check.

6. At length it was resolved to *tax* the Americans, to take away some of their money. This was first done in 1764. In that year, it was

ordered that the Americans should pay a certain sum on all the sugar, indigo, coffee, &c. which they should take from England to use in America.

7. In 1765, the English Parliament went still farther, and passed an act called the "*Stamp Act*," that is, a duty, or tax, on every piece of paper used for notes, deeds, wills, &c. It was called the "Stamp Act," because each piece of paper had a stamp upon it representing a crown.

8. This act was very odious to the Americans. They thought it unjust; and they resolved not to submit to it.

9. The next year, 1766, the act was repealed.

QUESTIONS.

1. When did the war of the Revolution begin? Why was it so called?
2. Until this time, to whom were the colonists in America subject? By whom had the country been settled? What right had the King, therefore?
3. How long were the colonists willing the King should govern them? How did they regard the English people? How the King? Who *was* the King?

4. How did the King and people in England regard the Americans? What did they fear?

5. Were the Americans prosperous? What was their numbers? What did the great men of England say?

6. What did they resolve to do? In what year was this? What was this year ordered? What act was passed id 1765? What was meant by the stamp act? Why was it so called?

8. What did the Americans think of this act? What did they resolve about it?

9. When was the act repealed?

STORY.

1. I have told you how odious and unjust the Americans thought the stamp act was; and it *was* unjust. The people in England had no right to take money from the Americans in this manner.

2. When the day arrived on which the stamp act was to take effect, the people in many parts of America met together, to show how much they disliked it.

3. I will tell you what took place in Boston. On that morning all the bells of the city were tolled, as if for a funeral. The merchants closed their stores, and the mechanics their shops. Then the people met in great numbers, and formed the image of a man. This image represented a *tory*. A tory was one who took part with England. Those who took part against England, and against the stamp act, were called *whigs*.

4. When they had formed this image, they dressed it up in clothes, and put a hat upon it, and raised it upon a pole.

5. They then carried it about the streets, and huzzaed, swinging their hats, and throwing stones. At length they hung it upon a gallows.

6. The people in England heard how the Americans felt, and how they acted; and the King and Parliament thought best to repeal the act. And they did wisely.

The Bostonians throwing the Tea overboard. p. 60.

LESSON XI.

WAR OF THE REVOLUTION.—DESTRUCTION OF TEA.

1. The stamp act was repealed, as I said, in 1766. This filled the Americans with joy. They thought the King and Parliament would tax them no more.

2. But they mistook. Not long after, they taxed them again in another way. They laid a tax on glass, paper, and *tea*. Several cargoes

of tea were sent to America. But the Americans resolved that they would buy none, because they would not pay the *tax* laid upon it.

3. One cargo of this tea was sent to Boston. When it arrived, the people resolved that it should not be landed. And now several persons assembled at the wharf, dressed like *Mohawk Indians*; and going on board the ship, they took three hundred and forty-two chests of tea, and *pitched the whole into the sea.* This was in the year 1773.

QUESTIONS.

1. When was the stamp act repealed? How did the Americans feel about it? What did they now think?

2. Did they think right? What did the King and Parliament soon after do? What articles did they tax? What did the people resolve about the tea sent over? Why?

3. To what place was one of the cargoes sent? When it arrived, what did the people resolve? What did they do with the tea? How were they dressed who threw the tea overboard? How many chests did they throw into the water? In what year was this?

STORY.

1. The destruction of the tea, about which I have told you, was a bold affair. It was an act of *open opposition* to the King and Parliament. Had the persons concerned in pitching it into the ocean been discovered, they would have come to harm. But each one kept his own secret, and that of his neighbour.

2. It was an act, too, of some *self-denial*. It was good tea, no doubt; and "*a good cup of tea*" of an afternoon, every one knows, is quite refreshing. At that day, tea was not as common as now; and when *first* brought to America, some persons, it is said, not knowing how to use it, *fried* it; but the proper mode of using it was soon discovered, and it became quite fashionable.

3. Tea-lovers would regret the loss of so much tea. But then their patriotism was stronger than their appetite. They would not drink tea, if they must be *slaves;* "no," said they—said all, "give us freedom, with only a cup of cold water."

4. Of the whole cargo, not a single chest—not even a *pound*, was saved. A small *phial* of it only was preserved, and that has been kept quite choice, and is now somewhere in Boston. A hundred years hence, what a curiosity will it be?

5. The above phial of tea was preserved in the following way: one of the persons who assisted in pitching the cargo into the ocean, found, on his return home, his *shoes* filled with it. This he put into a phial, sealed it, and so much has been preserved.

6. Another person present *designed* to save some, and filled one of his coat pockets. A companion near by saw what he was about, but said nothing. By and by, when the cargo was safely overboard, this person came softly up behind the other, and taking hold of the skirt of his coat, cut it off and threw it into the sea.

7. One of the chests thrown overboard happened not to break. Whether it was vexed at the treatment it had received in Boston, I shall not undertake to say. It soon *cleared* out of the harbour, and *coasting* along, floated into Dorchester. But here it was still worse treated. On its arrival, it was seized by some of the inhabitants, who carried it into the centre of the town, where, assembling a multitude of people, it was publicly *burned*.

8. Now, what sort of people do you think the people of the Revolution were? Who were ever bolder or more self-denying? The destruction of a cargo of tea, under some circumstances, would have been a small affair: the destruction of *that* cargo was an enterprise of great daring, and will tell well a thousand years to come.

Mr. Wheeler saving the public Flour from destruction. p. 67.

LESSON XII.

WAR OF THE REVOLUTION.—BATTLE OF LEXINGTON.

1. The destruction of the tea at Boston and other places, sorely vexed the people in England; and the King and Parliament sent ten thousand soldiers to America to make the people here behave better. This was in 1774.

2. The same year, men were sent from the eleven colonies to Philadelphia, to consult what

should be done. This was called the "Continental Congress." They agreed that no more goods should be brought from England, and none sent thither, until the King should treat the Americans more justly.

3. I must say a few things about this Congress. It was the first general Congress ever held in America. The men who composed it were distinguished for their courage and wisdom. I will add some verses, which were written by Judge Trumbull about them. You must learn them; they are very beautiful. If you do not now understand them, you will when you are older.

"Now meet the Fathers of the western clime,—
Nor names more noble graced the rolls of fame
When Spartan firmness braved the wrecks of time,
Or Latian virtue fann'd th' heroic flame.

"Not deeper thought th' immortal sage inspired
On Solon's* lips when Grecian Senates hung;
Nor manlier eloquence the bosom fired,
When genius thunder'd from the Athenian† tongue."

* A distinguished Grecian lawgiver. † Demosthenes, an eloquent orator of Athens.

4. The English soldiers sent to America were stationed at Boston. They were commanded by General Gage.

5. The Americans had placed some provisions, powder, and ball, at Concord, 18 miles north of Boston. These General Gage wished to destroy. He therefore sent eight hundred soldiers to Concord, to destroy them. These troops were commanded by Major Pitcairn, an English officer.

6. When these soldiers arrived at *Lexington*. on their way to Concord, some of the American people were seen standing near the meeting-house, with guns. Major Pitcairn told them "to disperse;" and when they would not disperse, he ordered his soldiers to fire, and eight were killed and others wounded.

7. This is called the "Battle of Lexington." The blood here shed was the first blood shed in the war of the revolution. The

battle took place April 19th, 1775. The war from this time began.

QUESTIONS.

1. How did the people in England feel about the destruction of the tea? How many soldiers were sent to America? For what purpose? In what year was this?

2. In what year did the Continental Congress meet? How many colonies sent delegates? Where did they meet? What did they agree upon?

3. What is said of this Congress? For what were the men who composed it distinguished? Can you repeat the verses written by Judge Trumbull about them?

4. Where were the English soldiers sent to America, stationed? Who commanded them?

5. Where had the Americans placed provisions, powder, and ball? Which way is Concord from Boston? How many miles? How many soldiers did General Gage send to destroy the provisions, powder, &c.? Who commanded them? Who was Major Pitcairn?

6. At what place did they meet some of the Americans with guns? What did Major Pitcairn bid these people do? Did they obey? What did he then bid his soldiers do? How many were killed?

7. What was this battle called? What is said of the blood here shed? In what year did this take place? In what month? On what day? When did the war begin?

STORY.

1. The enemy, after the battle of Lexington, proceeded to Concord, and there threw five hundred pounds of ball into the river and wells. They also destroyed about sixty barrels of flour. A considerable quantity of flour was saved by a Mr. Wheeler. The flour was stored in his barn.

Some of it was *his own*: the rest of it belonged to the public.

2. The British officers and soldiers, after searching several stores and barns, came to the barn of Mr. Wheeler. It was locked. A British officer told him to get the key and open it. He did so; when, lo! a large number of barrels of flour were in sight. The officer called his soldiers to come and destroy them.

3. "Sir," said Mr. Wheeler, putting his hand on to a barrel, "This is my flour. I am a miller, Sir. Yonder stands my mill. I get my living by it. In the winter, I grind a great deal of grain, and get it ready for market in the spring. This," pointing to one barrel, "is the flour of wheat; this," pointing to another, "is the flour of corn; this is the flour of rye. This," putting his hand on to his *own* casks, "is *my* flour, this is *my* wheat, this is *my* rye." He told the truth. The barrels upon which he put his hand, *were* his. The officer thought they were *all* his. He was under no obligation to undeceive him. What he said was the truth: this was right.

4. 'Well,' said the officer, 'we do not intend to injure *private* property.' Upon this, he turned and went out, leaving many barrels belonging to the public untouched.

5. I must add a word more about the battle of Lexing-

ton. The news of this battle spread. The country was filled with alarm and indignation. War was now certain. Hundreds shouldered their muskets all round the country, and hastened to Boston to assist in defending the country.

6. Every man was filled with zeal. The conduct of *General Putnam* may serve as an example of the zeal which was felt. He lived at Pomfret, in Connecticut, one hundred miles from Boston. When the news of the battle of Lexington reached Pomfret, he was ploughing in his field. He left his plough where it was, when the story was told him. Without changing his clothes, he mounted his horse, and in a single day was in the neighbourhood of Boston. This was the same General Putnam who once showed so much courage in killing a wolf.

The inhabitants of New-York pulling down the statue of George III. p. 73.

LESSON XIII.

WAR OF THE REVOLUTION.—BUNKER HILL—GENERAL WASHINGTON—INDEPENDENCE.

1. The battle of Lexington was fought, as I told you, April 19th, 1775. On the 17th of June, another battle was fought. This is called the "Battle of Bunker Hill." Bunker Hill is in the vicinity of Boston.

2. This was a hard fought battle. The Americans had only one hundred and fifteen

killed, and three hundred wounded. The British had more than two hundred killed, and more than eight hundred wounded. This was a great difference; but the Americans did not fire till the British were close at hand, and then they took good aim. General Putnam told the American soldiers how to manage. "Powder and ball are scarce," said he, "and you must not waste them. Don't fire till you can see the *whites* of their eyes—fire *low*—fire at their *waistbands*. You are all marksmen," said he; "you could kill a squirrel at a hundred yards. Take good aim—pick off the *handsome coats*." This they did, and the enemy fell by scores.

3. At length, however, the Americans were obliged to retreat, because they had used all their powder and ball. The battle showed the British what Yankees could do.

4. On the second of July, General Washington arrived at Cambridge, near Boston, and

took command of the American army. He was appointed commander-in-chief by the Continental Congress. He proved to be a great general, and was afterwards called the "Father of his country."

5. The next year, 1776, on the fourth day of July, the thirteen American colonies were declared "free and independent." This was done by the Continental Congress, at Philadelphia. Mr. Jefferson, afterwards President of the United States, wrote the Declaration. All the members of Congress signed it. This was a great event, because it declared to the world, that the Americans thought they ought to be free. It also showed their determination to be free and independent.

QUESTIONS.

1. When did the battle of Lexington occur? When the battle of Bunker Hill? Where is Bunker Hill?

2. How many Americans were killed in this battle? How many were wounded? How many of the British were killed? How many wounded? What did General Putnam tell the American soldiers?

3. Why were the Americans obliged to retreat? What did this battle show?

4. When did General Washington take command of the American army? Who appointed him commander-in-chief? What did he prove to be? What was he afterwards called?

5. When were the American colonies declared to be free and independent? By whom? Who wrote the Declaration? Who signed it? Why was this a great event?

STORY.

1. The fourth of July, every child knows, is called "*Independence Day.*" It is a great day in almost every town in the United States. No wonder it should be thought a great day—no wonder every one should rejoice—because on that day, in 1776, the Americans declared that George III. the King of England, should rule over them no more.

2. It was a bold act to declare the colonies free and independent. Had those who signed the Declaration been taken by the British, they would have been hung. This they well knew. But they were brave and steadfast men. They loved their country, and were willing to hazard their lives for her good.

3. After they had signed the Declaration, it was printed, and thousands of copies were sent abroad, into every part of the country. Great rejoicings took place everywhere—

all the bells were rung, in token of joy—cannon were fired, and large bonfires were kindled.

4. I must tell you what the people in New-York did. In a certain spot, in that city, there stood a large statue or representation of King George III. It was made of lead. In one hand, he held a sceptre, or a kind of sword; and on his head, he wore a crown.

5. When the news of the Declaration of Independence reached the city, a great multitude were seen running to this statue. Soon the cry was heard from a hundred voices, "Down with it—down with it," and soon a rope was placed about its neck, and the leaden King George "came tumbling down."

5. I shall only add, that when the statue was fairly down, it was cut to pieces, and converted into musket balls, to kill the soldiers whom his majesty had sent over to fight the Americans.

The English officer questioning Mrs. Darrah. p. 79.

LESSON XIV.

RETREAT OF WASHINGTON—BATTLES OF TRENTON, BRANDYWINE, AND GERMANTOWN.

1. Congress declared the colonies free and independent July 4th, 1776. The war, however, lasted for several years; and all this time the Americans were fighting to effect their independence, and to drive the British from the country.

2. But *now* a gloomy time came on. This was in the fall of 1776. General Washington's army was reduced to three thousand men. He was obliged to retreat from Long Island into New-Jersey, and afterwards into Pennsylvania. During this retreat, the army suffered greatly. The soldiers had poor provisions, and not enough of them. They had few blankets, and few shoes. The ground over which they passed was often stained with their blood.

3. In December, however, things looked brighter. General Washington and his army came back into New-Jersey, and there was fought the "battle of Trenton." The Americans took a thousand prisoners. These prisoners were "Hessians." They came from a place called Hesse, in Germany.

4. The next year—that is, in 1777—in September, was fought the "battle of Brandywine," in Delaware. Another battle was

fought in October. This was the "battle of Germantown," six miles from Philadelphia. In both these battles the Americans lost ground.

5. The season was now growing late. After the battle of Germantown, the British army went to Philadelphia, where they spent the winter. The American army spent the winter fifteen miles from Philadelphia.

6. This was a trying winter for the American army. Three thousand were sick at one time. Once they were in danger of famine. The soldiers were obliged to lie in their tents, without blankets; and to walk in the snow, and on frozen ground, without shoes.

QUESTIONS.

1. When was independence declared? Did the war continue after this? Why did the Americans fight?

2. What is said of the state of things in the fall of 1776? To what number was the American army reduced? Where was General Washington obliged to retreat? Did the army suffer? For what?

3. When did things become brighter? What battle was fought? How

many prisoners were taken by the Americans? What were they called? From what country did they come?

4. When was the battle of Brandywine fought? Where is Brandywine? When the battle of Germantown? Where is Germantown? What was the success of the Americans in these battles?

5. Where did the British army spend the winter? Where the American army?

6. What is said of the American army this winter? How many were sick at one time? Of what were they in danger? From what other causes did they suffer?

STORY.

1. I will now tell you a story about *Lydia Darrah*. She and her husband, whose name was William, lived in Philadelphia.

2. At the time the event happened, which I am about relating, the British army were in Philadelphia. The American army were encamped a short distance from it.

3. A British officer lodged in the house of William and Lydia Darrah. One day, the officer told Lydia that he expected two other officers to make him a visit that evening—that they would stay late—that she and her family might all go to bed; and that when the officers were going away, he would call her to let them out.

4. In the evening, the officers came. Lydia sent all her family early to bed. But she could not sleep herself. She

felt anxious, and suspected mischief. She could not help listening.

5. The officers were talking about attacking General Washington and his army, by surprise, two nights from that time. She heard this, went down, and flung herself upon the bed. The officer sometime after called ; but she did not come. A second and a third time he called, and each time louder, for he thought she was asleep. At length he descended, and knocked at her door, soon after which she came, unbarred the door of the hall, and the officers went away.

6. She now felt distressed. What should she do? She durst not tell the secret to any one, not even to her husband. The next day her plan was formed. The family were in want of flour ; so she told William that *she* would go and get some. William said no, that he would go. But Lydia wished so much to go, that he consented ; and yet he thought it strange that his wife should wish to go and purchase flour.

7. Lydia now taking a bag, went to General Howe, the chief general of the British army, and told him she wished to go to a certain mill, out of the city, to buy some flour, and asked him to give her leave to pass the British troops. This he readily did.

8. When she reached the mill, she left her bag, and hastened on till she saw an American officer. "Sir," said she, "I wish to tell you a secret." And then she told what she had heard the British officers say. "Go," said she, "to General Washington, tell it to him, and bid him be ready for the enemy, but don't betray me."

9. Lydia now returned to the mill, took her flour, and reached home in safety. The night appointed for the expedition arrived. The British troops were silently marched out of the city, and went to attack the American army. On their arrival, General Washington was prepared. Every cannon was loaded, and the troops marshalled for battle. The British were afraid to attack him, and returned to Philadelphia.

10. The evening after their return, the British officer called Lydia to his room, and with some sternness, said, "Lydia, we have been betrayed!"

11. 'Betrayed, sir!' exclaimed she, with seeming surprise, 'who could betray you?' "I know not who it was," replied the officer—his keen eye settling steadily upon the modest countenance of Lydia—"some of your family, perhaps."

12. 'Sir,' said Lydia, 'you bid me send them all early to bed, and I obeyed you.' "Are you sure that no one of

them was up?—*You* was asleep, I well know; for I had to call several times, and even to knock at your door, before I could awake you—but your family—"

13. 'Sir,' said Lydia, 'I assure you that they were all asleep—I am certain; for I sent them all early to bed, as you told me.'

13. "Well," said the officer, "I know not who betrayed us—but this I know, that we found General Washington prepared to receive us; and we have marched back, like a parcel of fools."

General Putnam escaping down the stone steps at Horseneck. p. 84.

LESSON XV.

WAR OF THE REVOLUTION.—BATTLE OF SARATOGA—MONMOUTH—BURNING OF FAIRFIELD.

1. I WILL now tell you of an event which spread great joy throughout America. This was the "*battle of Saratoga.*" Saratoga lies north of Albany, in the state of New-York. A part of the American army was near this place. It was commanded by General Gates.

2. Towards this place, a British army came from Canada. It was commanded by General Burgoyne. Here, in October, 1771, these two armies met. A battle ensued. The Americans were victorious. The whole British army surrendered, and became prisoners. They amounted to five thousand and seven hundred men. This surrender was a joyful event. It took place on the seventeenth day of the month.

3. The next year, 1778, in June, was fought the "*battle of Monmouth.*" Monmouth lies sixty-four miles from Philadelphia. It was a severe contest. The day was so hot, that the tongues of the soldiers swelled out of their mouths. In this battle the Americans gained some advantage.

4. In the following year, 1779, a party of British came into Connecticut, and plundered *New-Haven*, where Yale College is situated. They burned *Fairfield* and *Norwalk*, and some

other places. Fairfield was burned just at evening. A thunder storm came up at the same time, and added greatly to the horrors of the scene.

QUESTIONS.

1. What event spread great joy through America? Where does Saratoga lie? Who commanded this part of the American army?

2. From what place did the British army come? Who commanded them? When did the two armies meet? What ensued? Who were victorious? Who surrendered? How many surrendered? On what day did this take place?

3. In what year was the battle of Monmouth fought? What month? How far is Monmouth from Philadelphia? What is said of the day on which this battle was fought? Who gained the advantage?

4. When did a party of the British come into Connecticut? What city did they plunder? What town did they burn? At what time in the day was Fairfield burned? What circumstance added to the horrors of the scene?

STORY.

1. I will now tell you two stories—one about *General Putnam*, and the other about *General Washington*.

2. Soon after the British burned Norwalk, they went to Horseneck. This place lies on Long-Island Sound, about thirty miles from New-York. General Putnam was here, with one hundred and fifty men, and two cannon. The British amounted to fifteen hundred men.

3. General Putnam was a bold man. He placed his cannon on a hill, near the meeting-house; and as the British advanced, the cannon were fired. At length, the enemy came so near, that he told his men to escape into a swamp near by.

4. He himself was on horseback. It seemed impossible that he should escape. The hill was very steep, and down that no horse could go, only in the direction in which the British were coming.

5. Putnam bethought himself. He had but a moment to think. He saw some stone steps. There were one hundred of them. The people had laid them in order to ascend the hill to the meeting-house.

6. It is life, or death, thought Putnam, and down he rode. On came the British. They were sure of him. But when they arrived at the spot, they saw Putnam galloping at a distance from the hill. They were afraid to follow down the steps. They sent some bullets after him; however, but one touched him, and that one went only through his hat.

7. My other story is about General Washington. What I shall relate happened, I believe, at a time when a part of the American army was at West Point. West Point lies on the Hudson, sixty miles above New-York.

8. Not far from this place, a gentleman lived, whom General Washington frequently visited. He had been a tory; but now pretended to be a real friend to America.

9. One day, General Washington was at his house. "Will you do me the favour, General," said he, "to dine with me to-morrow afternoon?" 'With all my heart,' said General Washington. "Come at two," said he; "please be punctual; and for once, General, leave your guard at home: come like a real friend."

10. The next day, at *one o'clock*, General Washington mounted his horse, and, taking a bye road, in half an hour came to the house. The gentleman was glad to see him. "You are quite punctual," said he—"and all alone?" 'Yes,' replied the General, 'no one with me.'

11. Dinner was not yet ready. General Washington and the gentleman took a walk abroad. At some distance, they saw a party of horsemen approaching. 'What can this mean?' asked Washington. The troop came nearer—they were dressed in *British* uniform. 'Bless me!' said Washington, 'what can this mean?' at the same time looking at his friend.

12. "Oh!" said the gentleman, "they seem to be a party of light horse. I believe they are *British;* but they probably mean no harm." General Washington stood

calm and collected. In a few minutes they came up, and the party dismounted.

13. As they approached, the gentleman stepped up to General Washington, and tapping him on the shoulder, said, "*General, you are my prisoner.*" 'No!' said General Washington—'*you are mine.* These, sir, are *my* men. I directed them to put on British uniform—I directed them to be here *before your party arrived.* You are *my* prisoner. And now, soldiers,' said he, 'take this *false friend* to the American camp.'

14. He *was* accordingly taken to the American camp. But General Washington humanely forgave him, and released him, upon condition that he should leave the country for ever.

15. I shall only add, that this man had been bribed to act the part he did, by the promise of an immense sum of money. General Washington suspected mischief, by his being requested to come *precisely at two o'clock*, and to come *without his guard.* Who this gentleman was, I know not, but the story we believe to be true.

Capture of Major Andre. p. 91.

LESSON XVI.

WAR OF THE REVOLUTION.—BATTLE OF CAMDEN—FRENCH FLEET—ARNOLD'S CONSPIRACY.

1. We shall now hasten rapidly to the conclusion of the war. After the year 1779, the principal theatre of the war was in the *southern* colonies.

2. In August, 1780, occurred the "*battle of Camden*," in South-Carolina. Camden lies one hundred and twenty miles north-west from

Charleston. It was a bloody battle, and very distressing to the Americans.

3. A short time before the battle of Camden, a party of British entered *New-Jersey*, and wickedly burned several villages. At one place, called "*Connecticut Farms*," a British soldier walked up to the windows of the minister's house, and shot his wife in the midst of her little family.

4. In July, an encouraging event occurred. This was the arrival in Rhode-Island of a fleet of men-of-war from France, with six thousand French soldiers, to help the Americans in the war.

5. The next month, September, a very base plot was discovered, which came well nigh ruining America. This was no other than a plan to deliver *West Point* into the hands of the British. This plan was formed by *General Arnold*, who commanded at West Point, and

Major Andre, a British officer. But General Washington discovered the plot, and defeated it. Arnold escaped; but Andre was taken, and hung as a spy. Arnold was a traitor, and for ever disgraced his name.

QUESTIONS.

1. After the year 1779, where was the war chiefly carried on?

2. In what year did the battle of Camden occur? In what state is Camden? How far from Charleston? Which way? What is said of this battle?

3. What is said of a party of British who entered New-Jersey a little before the battle of Camden? What took place at Connecticut Farms?

4. What force arrived in America in July to help on the war? How many men came from France?

5. What plot was discovered in September? What was the design of this plot? Who formed it? Who discovered and defeated it? What became of Arnold? What of Andre? What was Arnold?

STORY.

1. You will like to hear more about General Arnold and Major Andre.

2. General Arnold, I told you, was in command of West Point, an important fortress on Hudson River, 60 miles above New-York. The importance of this post the British

well understood, and secretly offered Arnold thirty thousand pounds sterling to deliver it into their hands.

3. But could an American officer, an American *patriot*, be bribed? Arnold was no patriot. He had conducted improperly some time before, and by order of a court-martial, General Washington had reprimanded him. This he so much resented, that in anger he left the army, and determined upon revenge.

4. At length, he *pretended* to regret his conduct; he said he wished to serve his country—he wished to shew his patriotism, and he begged that he might have the command of West Point.

5. This was all *pretence*. His heart was black, his intentions base. General Washington suspected him not—no one suspected his object, and the command of West Point was given to him.

6. No sooner had he taken the command of this post, than he wrote to the British general in New-York to send some one, with whom he might arrange matters to deliver it up.

7. The British general revealed the secret to Major Andre, a young officer in the British army, who sailed up the river in a sloop of war called the *Vulture*. On his arrival near West Point, he and Arnold had an interview,

under cover of night, and there did the infamous American general agree to deliver up the fortress—*there* plotted the ruin of his country.

8. A merciful Providence, however, defeated the plan. Andre attempted to return to New-York by land. On the way, he was seized by three American soldiers, to whom he offered all he had to be released. But they were not to be bribed. They took him to an American officer in the neighbourhood, and by him he was delivered to Washington.

9. Andre was in the morning of life—"fair, graceful, and accomplished." But for this *one* deed of infamy, his character was without reproach. It was painful for the court-martial which tried him to condemn him; but he was a *spy*, and they felt obliged by their oath to pronounce him guilty. It was painful for Washington to sign his death-warrant—but this *duty* required.

10. That was a sorrowful day through all the American army, when Andre was hung. But according to the rules of war, it could not be otherwise. It would not do to pardon him. All knew this—all felt it—yet many were the tears which were shed by officers and soldiers, when the noble and manly form of Andre ascended the scaffold to be hung.

11. Had it been *Arnold*, no tears would have been shed. But a mysterious Providence suffered that guilty man to escape. He fled to New-York, and entered the British service, to fight against his country.

12. Before Andre's death, Washington was bent on taking Arnold; and could he effect this, he might, perhaps, secure the pardon of the former.

13. Arnold, I said, was in New-York. Washington thought of a plan, and when he had matured it, he sent for an officer by the name of Major Lee.

14. "Lee," said he, as that officer entered, "read these papers—they will inform you of a plan by which I hope to take Arnold, and save Andre." When Major Lee had finished reading the papers, Washington inquired, "Do you know a man who is qualified—one who can be trusted?"

15. Lee thought, and replied, he did. His name was *Champe*—he was a serjeant—he was honest, and brave, and persevering. "Well," said Washington, "go and tell him the plan—tell him of the trust reposed in him—tell him of the danger—tell him that I will reward him."

16. Champe hesitated—but at length consented; and that very night was on his way towards New-York, urging forward a fleet horse to escape, if possible, any who might pursue him as a deserter.

17. Champe was pursued by a party hastily formed for that purpose. He had been seen secretly leaving the camp, and the captain of the day took him for a deserter. Lee could not well reveal the secret, and as Champe had the start, he bid the party take him if they could.

18. Champe, I said, fled. He thought he might be pursued, and he went as on the wings of the wind. In the morning, the pursuing party saw him at a distance, and pressed on with redoubled speed. Champe saw them coming, and pressed on still more rapidly; on arriving at the river, he leaped from his horse into the water—swam to a boat, on board of which he was taken to a British vessel, and conveyed to New-York.

19. Here he found where Arnold lodged, and one dark night had contrived a plan to seize him, and convey him across the Hudson, where Lee was to be in readiness to conduct him to Washington.

20. Before the time arrived, however, Arnold was safe. He had suddenly, and to Champe unexpectedly, changed his quarters, in order to go on board a vessel sailing with troops to Virginia.

21. On board a vessel, Champe sailed at the same time, as a soldier in the British service. But on arriving in Virginia, he deserted, and returned to the American army.

Washington did as he had promised, and Champe was permitted to leave the army, with a handsome reward.

22. I shall only add respecting Arnold, that after the war he went to England, where in 1801 he died, justly despised, not only in America, the land of his birth, but even in all England, by every one who laid any claim to the character of a patriot and an honourable man.

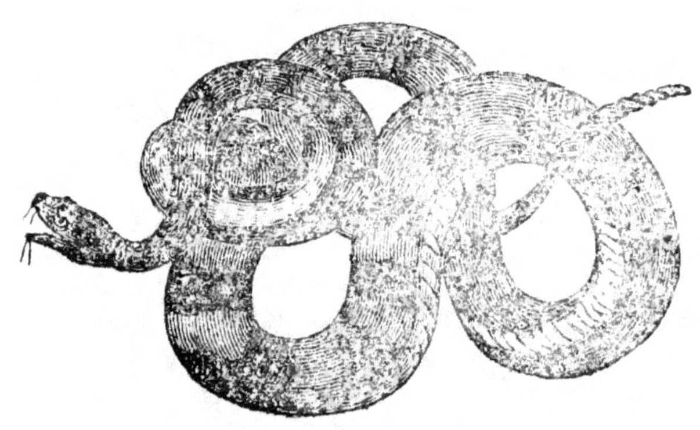

General Washington taking leave of his officers. p. 98.

LESSON XVII.

WAR OF THE REVOLUTION.—BATTLE OF YORKTOWN—BURNING OF NEW-LONDON—PEACE.

1. On the nineteenth of October, 1781, the great "*battle of Yorktown*" was fought. Yorktown is a small village on York River, in Virginia.

2. In this battle, Lord Cornwallis commanded the British. General Washington commanded the Americans. Every thing was now

at stake. If the Americans could prove victorious in *this* battle, they might be free and independent.

3. They *were* victorious. They had the joy to see seven thousand British soldiers lay down their arms, and Lord Cornwallis surrender his sword to General Washington.

4. This was a great triumph for the Americans, and spread joy throughout all the land.

5. While things were going on so prosperously for the Americans at Yorktown, a sad event took place in Connecticut. General Arnold came from New-York, in a vessel, with troops—took fort Trumbull and fort Griswold. The American troops in this latter fort were cruelly put to death, and New-London was burned.

6. The war now ended. Peace was made November 30, 1782. In 1783, November 3, the American army was disbanded. December

23, General Washington resigned his commission as commander-in-chief of the American armies.

QUESTIONS.

1. When did the battle of Yorktown take place? Where is Yorktown?
2. In this battle, who commanded the British? Who commanded the Americans?
3. Who were victorious? How many British soldiers laid down their arms?
4. What is said of this triumph?
5. What sad event took place about this time in Connecticut? What forts were taken? What troops were butchered? What town was burned?
6. When was peace made? When was the American army disbanded? When did General Washington resign his commissions?

STORY.

1. Thus ended a long and distressing war. The Americans had suffered much. Many a brave soldier, and a brave officer, had gone to their graves. But the people were now free and independent.

2. General Washington had done himself immortal honour, and so had La Fayette, and Putnam, and Gates, and many others, who had fought with him.

3. It was a trying time, when General Washington took leave of the army. The soldiers loved him, and many a tear was shed when he bid them adieu.

4. It was a trying time, too, when he took leave of his officers. He met them at New-York. He entered the room where they were. He called for a glass of wine; and while he held it in his hand, and before he drank it, he said, "Companions in arms! with love and gratitude I now take my leave of you. May your latter days be as prosperous and happy as your former ones have been glorious and honourable."

5. Taking them by the hand, he bade them farewell. They followed him to the side of the Hudson; and, as he entered the boat which was to convey him away, tears rolled down his cheeks, and down theirs. Waving his hand as he departed, he bade them a silent adieu.

6. Another trying hour soon came. He appeared in the Hall of Congress, and laid his commission upon the table. This was the greatest and noblest action of his life. Men generally feel reluctant to surrender power. He did it with pleasure—did it nobly—and having done it, hastened to his house, at Mount Vernon, in Virginia.

General Washington and the Irishman. p. 102.

LESSON XVIII.

FEDERAL CONSTITUTION—WASHINGTON, PRESIDENT.

1. The war now being over, and the people being free and independent, they had a right to govern themselves.

2. September 17, 1787, the "*Federal Constitution*" was adopted. A constitution is a body of rules, by which people are governed.

It was called "*Federal*," because the several states *united* or *leagued* together to adopt it.

3. General Washington was elected the first President. John Adams was elected Vice-President.

4. On the 30th April, 1789, General Washington was inducted into office, in the presence of Congress and of a multitude of spectators.

5. General Washington continued in office eight years. Under his administration, the United States, as they were now called, greatly flourished; and when he retired, it was said of him, "That he was first in war—first in peace—first in the hearts of his countrymen."

QUESTIONS.

1. The war being over, what right had the people?
2. When was the Federal Constitution adopted? What is a Constitution? Why was it called Federal?
3. Who was elected first President? Who Vice-President?
4. When was General Washington inducted into office?
5. How long did he continue in office? Did the country flourish while he was President? What was said of him, when he retired?

STORY.

1. I have told you something about General Washington. I could tell you much more. You ought to know, if you do not already know, that he was as much beloved as a President, as he was as a general of the army.

2. He was a man of great kindness, and took much pleasure in doing good to the old revolutionary soldiers. He never turned away from any one, however poor.

3. I will tell you how he one day treated an old soldier who came to see him. It was on a certain day, called *levee* day; that is, when *great persons* call to pay their respects to the President.

4. Just about the time the company were expected, an Irishman rapped at the door. The porter stood ready to open the door, expecting to admit some very distinguished man; when lo! an Irishman stood before him. He was a sad object to look at, but he had been a soldier in the revolutionary war, and he had come to pay General Washington a visit.

5. "Is his honour at home?" asked the Irishman. 'Yes,' replied the porter, 'but you cannot see him: he is expecting company.' "Well!" said Pat, "I suppose I may come in?" 'No, you shall not come in.' "But I will come in"—and in he walked, and took a seat.

6. The company soon arrived—Ministers of state, and

Senators, and Judges—the great men and the gay; and there sat Pat, the whole time, with his hat under his arm, looking about, and thinking as how it was the finest company he was ever in.

7. No one disturbed him, and he disturbed no one. At length, the company retired; upon which the porter told the President that there was an obstinate Irishman there. "Some old soldier, probably," said the President. "Let me see him."

8. The Irishman rose, as his old general approached, and roared out, "Long life to your honour's excellency!" at the same time he swung his hat, and, at length, hurled it on to the floor, and stood as straight and precise as he once did on the battle ground.

9. "May it plase your honour," said Pat, "I was once your honour's soldier, and I have marched under your honour's orders, and many's the hard knock I have had too; and I was wounded in the battle of Germantown, may it plase your honour; but they didn't kill me, for I believe I am alive yet—Hurra for America!—Hurra for Washington!—and it does my heart good to see your honour once more. And how is the dear leddy and the little ones?"

10. Washington could contain himself no longer. He laughed heartily; and thanked Pat for inquiring about

Mrs. Washington, who, he said, was well; but as for the little ones, unfortunately he had none.

11. "Bless your honour," said Pat, "and I wish you had a thousand, and that they were all like your honour's self." Well did Washington know what Pat was after; and slipping a piece of money into his hand, he retired—"Hurra for Washington!" said Pat, as he put it into his pocket.

12. Having recovered his hat, he took up his line of march for the door; and as he passed the porter, he pulled from his pocket the money, and called out, "There, now, you *Hessian!* see how his honour's excellence remembers an old soldier. Hurra for Washington!"

Mrs. Fries supplicating President Adams to pardon her Husband. p. 109.

LESSON XIX.

JOHN ADAMS, PRESIDENT.

1. In 1797, Gen. Washington declined being President again. John Adams was now chosen President, and Thomas Jefferson Vice-President.

2. The state of the country, at the time Mr. Adams was elected President, was prosperous. But soon after, France threatened to make war upon the United States.

3. War being expected, Congress ordered an army to be raised, and appointed General Washington to command it. The difficulty, however, was settled, and the army reduced.

4. On the 14th December, 1799, General Washington died. This event filled the country with gloom. Every one felt that he himself had sustained a great loss.

5. In 1800, the city of Washington became the seat of government. Before this time, Congress had met in the city of Philadelphia.

6. In 1801, Mr. Adams' term of office as President expired; and Thomas Jefferson was chosen President in his room. Aaron Burr was chosen Vice-President.

QUESTIONS.

1. When was John Adams chosen President? Who was chosen Vice-President?

2. What was the state of the country at this time? What nation soon after threatened the United States with war?

3. What did Congress do upon this? Whom did they appoint to command the army? What took place, however?

4. When did General Washington die? What is said of this event?

5. When did the city of Washington become the seat of government?

6. When was Mr. Jefferson chosen President? Who was chosen Vice-President?

STORY.

1. I have two stories to tell about this elder President Adams. The one relating to his *courage:* the other to his *humanity*—both excellent traits in any man's character.

2. In the year 1778, while the War of the Revolution was still going on, Congress appointed Mr. Adams ambassador to France. A frigate, called the *Boston*, was fitted out to convey him to that country. The commander was a brave man, by the name of Capt. Tucker.

3. The ocean, at that time, was thronged with British armed vessels, watching for American ships. A voyage, therefore, was attended with no small hazard.

4. A few days after sailing, a British ship of war was discovered. The sight of her caused no ordinary emotions in the breast of Capt. Tucker. But it was not fear—no! fear was a stranger there. "Oh!" thought he, "what an opportunity to do my country honour!"

5. Mr. Adams perceived the workings of his patriotic spirit. 'Do you wish to fight her?' asked the ambassador. "With all my heart," replied the animated captain. "Had I your leave, we would soon be down upon her." 'Well, captain,' said the ambassador, 'you *have* my leave; we will *all* share the honour in the brush.'

6. "Ah! your excellency," exclaimed the captain, "there's the rub. My orders are to convey you safely. There must be no fighting, unless you go below." 'Below! below!' exclaimed the ambassador, '*I* go below! Well, I will go below—but—'

7. The captain knew not the spirit of the man he carried, and now scarcely attended to any thing but getting his vessel ready for action. Every sail was immediately spread—every gun was loaded and manned.

8. The battle opened at a distance, and as the ships neared each other, the broadsides were more frequent, while smaller arms filled up the intervals. Mr. Adams sat in the cabin peaceably for a time; but, at length, the action growing warm, he could stay—he would stay—no longer; he rushed on deck; he seized a musket, and was doing his duty like a hero with the men, when he was discovered by Capt. Tucker.

9. "What!" exclaimed the latter—"your excellency

here? you promised to stay below. Shall I *order* you away?" 'Yes, if you please,' said Mr. Adams, 'but I will fight while I stay.' And well he did fight: but the Captain said it would not do, and when Mr. Adams, at length, *refused* to retire, the resolute captain seized him, and bore him in his arms by force to the cabin.

10. My other story about Mr. Adams, relates to his humanity. The incident occurred while he was President.

11. A certain man, by the name of John Fries, had been concerned with others in an insurrection in Pennsylvania, and on a charge of treason was tried and condemned to death. This sentence, Mr. Adams, as President, approved.

12. Fries was an old man. He had a wife and ten children. Several of the childen were small—one was an infant at the breast. It was thought a pity by many in Philadelphia, that a man so old, with a family so dependent, should be hung.

13. It was accordingly agreed to send a petition abroad among the inhabitants to be signed, begging the President to pardon the aged offender. The petition circulated, and several thousands added their names to it.

14. When ready, the petition was handed to Mrs. Fries, who with her infant in her arms, and her nine children, all were seen going to present it to President Adams.

15. Being invited in, they entered the room where the President sat; and ere he was aware, the afflicted mother and all her children were on their knees before him. She presented the petition; she begged him to spare her husband: and the children sobbing, begged him to spare their father.

16. It was a moment of surpassing interest. He cast his eye over the petition—he looked round upon the prostrate, supplicating group. Tears gushed from his eyes. He rose—raised his hands to heaven—rushed from the room to his closet, and seizing a pen, wrote a full and free pardon, which he presented to the grateful wife and her now happy children.

The life of Lieutenant Decatur saved by a sailor. p. 117.

LESSON XX.

THOMAS JEFFERSON, PRESIDENT.

1. IN 1801, as I said, Mr. Jefferson became President of the United States. He continued in office eight years.

2. In 1804, a sad event event took place. This was a *duel* which was fought between Colonel Burr, Vice-President of the United States, and General Hamilton, who was a

highly distinguished man, and much respected by many people in the United States. General Hamilton was killed.

3. In 1805, peace was made between the United States and Tripoli, a country in Africa, lying in the Mediterranean Sea. This people had done much injury to the Americans, in taking vessels in the Mediterranean Sea belonging to American merchants, and in abusing their crews.

4. In 1806, Colonel Burr, who had killed General Hamilton, attempted to set up a new government in the southern part of the United States. He intended that New-Orleans should be his seat of government. But his plan was found out, and he was tried. Almost every one believed him guilty; but it could not be proved, and he was released.

5. About this time, 1806, France and England were at *war* with each other; and both

did all in their power to injure the United States. They were very jealous of the people here, and tried to provoke a quarrel with them.

6. In 1807, June 22d, a British frigate, called the *Leopard*, attacked the American frigate *Chesapeake*, and killed three men. The attack was made, because, it was said by the British, on board the Chesapeake were some of their men. This attack roused the Americans ; and things now began to look like war.

7. On the 2d of July, Mr. Jefferson issued a proclamation, forbidding any ships of war from England to enter the harbours of the United States, till England should make satisfaction for the attack upon the Chesapeake.

8. At this time, Mr. Monroe, who was afterwards President of the United States, was Minister to England. Letters were written to him, to *demand* satisfaction of the English government.

9. As difficulties, however, seemed to increase, Mr. Jefferson directed Congress to meet at Washington, Oct. 27th, to determine what was best to be done. When Congress met, it was deemed prudent to equip one hundred thousand of the militia, to build eighty or ninety gun-boats, and to build and repair fortifications.

10. After a little time, these measures were thought insufficient. On the 22d of December, therefore, an *embargo* was laid on all vessels in port, by which they were forbidden to depart.

11. But even an embargo was found insufficient. This, therefore, was repealed March 1st, 1809; and, at the same time, a *non-intercourse* law was passed, by which it was ordained, that no more trade, either with England or France, should be carried on, till difficulties were settled.

12. Such was the state of things on the 4th of March, 1809, when Mr. Jefferson retired from office. James Madison was chosen to succeed him as President; and George Clinton was elected Vice-President.

QUESTIONS.

1. When did Mr. Jefferson become President of the United States? How long did he continue in office?
2. In 1804, what sad event took place? Who was killed?
3. In 1805, what peace was made? Where is Tripoli? What injury had the people of that country done?
4. In 1806, what did Col. Burr attempt to set up? What place was to be the capital of his government? What is said of his plan? Why was he released?
5. What is said of France and England in 1806? How did they treat the United States? How long did he continue in office? Why did they treat them thus?
6. What took place in 1807? Why was this attack made? How did the Americans feel about this?
7. When did Mr. Jefferson issue a proclamation? What did the proclamation forbid?
8. Who was at this time minister to England? What was he directed to do?
9. Whom did Mr. Jefferson call together? Why? Where? What did Congress do?
10. What next took place? When was the embargo laid? What is meant by an embargo? Why was it laid?
11. Did the embargo answer the purpose for which it was laid? What became of it? What was enacted in its place? What did the non-intercourse law order?
12. When did Mr. Jefferson retire from office? Who succeeded him? Who became Vice-President?

STORY.

1. The lesson which you have now learned would furnish me with several interesting stories, had I time to relate them. I might give you some particulars about the duel between Col. Burr and Gen. Hamilton. This was truly a sad piece of business. Col. Burr was Vice-President of the United States. Gen. Hamilton had been aid to Gen. Washington during the war, and had filled several offices of distinction.

2. Both were great men. Both might have been useful for many years. What a bad example they set! What a crime did they commit! Gen. Hamilton was killed. Every one thought him to be a foolish man. As to Col. Burr, few have either loved or respected him since. Who can love or respect a duellist?

3. I might tell an interesting story, also, about the war with Tripoli. I can give, however, only a few particulars.

4. Tripoli lies, as I have said, on the coast of Africa. The people of that country are much like the Algerines, about whose cruel piracies almost every one has heard.

5. For a long time the Tripolitan cruisers, as they were called, had ill-treated merchant vessels from America. These vessels were often taken, their cargoes were plundered, and the crews sold into slavery.

6. In 1803, Commodore Preble was sent with a fleet, to chastise the people of Tripoli. Soon after he sailed, Capt. Bainbridge was sent in the frigate Philadelphia, to assist him. On the arrival of the latter, a piratical vessel from Tripoli was chased into the harbour of Tripoli. Unfortunately, the Philadelphia grounded, and Capt. Bainbridge and his crew were taken and carried to Tripoli, where they were loaded with irons, and thrust into a dungeon.

7. Lieutenant Decatur, afterwards Commodore Decatur, was at this time with Commodore Preble. Desirous of distinguishing himself, by permission he took a boat called a Xebec, and with twenty men sailed for the Philadelphia, to set her on fire.

8. It was now night. Many Tripolitans had been placed on board the Philadelphia, as a guard. And as the Xebec approached, they cried, "Who is there?"

9. A man on board the Xebec, who could speak in the language of the people of Tripoli, replied—'We've no anchor, let us make fast to the frigate, or we shall be blown away.'

10. "You may make fast to the *hawser*," said they, "till we can ask leave of the Admiral." The hawser is a kind of rope, or cable. This being done, a boat put off from the Philadelphia to ask permission of the Admiral for the boat to be made fast to the frigate.

11. No sooner had the boat gone, however, than Lieut. Decatur and his men leaped on board the Philadelphia. Oh! what a scene soon took place! What carnage was there! In a few minutes, fifty Tripolitans were reeking in blood on the deck. Not one escaped. The vessel was set on fire, and the flames rose.

12. And as they rose, the Americans leaped into their boat, and all but two returned in safety to Commodore Preble. One American was killed, and one was wounded. The sailor who was wounded, was a brave, generous tar. He saved the life of Decatur. The latter accidentally fell, and a sabre was coming down upon him--a moment longer, and he would have been no more. The sailor leaped forward, extended his arm, and took the blow himself. It severed his arm, but it saved the life of his brave commodore.

13. I will only add, that in consequence of the burning of the Philadelphia, the sufferings of Capt. Bainbridge and his crew were much increased. But not long after, the war was brought to a close by Gen. Eaton; and a treaty of peace was made, by which all American prisoners were released.

14. My little readers would like, no doubt, also to read some particulars about the plan of Col. Burr, after he had

killed Gen. Hamilton, to form a new government. I wish I had room for the story. It was a wicked plot which he contrived: it was what is called *treason.* But it could not be *proved,* and he was released.

15. I have time to add only a few lines about Mr. Jefferson. Different opinions exist about him as a President. But all unite in praising him for one thing, the *Declaration of Independence.* This he wrote. It was a bold, manly, and noble production. It will add honour to his name, while America lasts.

16. The Declaration was written in 1776. It was read and adopted July 4th, of that year. And the man who urged its adoption, who pressed it forward, more than any other, was *John Adams.*

17. Now mark a wonderful circumstance. Just fifty years from that year—from that day—these two men died—died within two or three hours of each other—died while the people in all parts of the United States were celebrating independence.

18. This was a wonderful coincidence! It was thought so here. It was thought so in England. And in that country, some said it was almost too wonderful to be true. But it *was* true, wonderful as it did appear.

19. Fifty-six men signed the Declaration of Indepen-

dence. Now but one of them all remains—Charles Carroll, of Carollton, in Maryland. The rest moulder under ground. He lives, an old man—may he yet live for years. But though death must come to him—to all, as years roll away—may it not come to American Liberty, till time shall be no longer.

A British Midshipman receiving a severe wound. p. 127.

LESSON XXI.

JAMES MADISON, PRESIDENT.—WAR WITH ENGLAND.

1. Mr. Madison became President on the 4th of March, 1809, and continued in office eight years.

2. The difficulties between the United States and England, which began while Mr. Jefferson was President, still continued, and became

still more serious. Some attempts were made to settle them, but without effect.

3. In May, 1811, these difficulties were much increased by an attack of a British sloop-of-war, called the *Little Belt*, upon the American frigate *President*. This was an unprovoked attack, and filled the Americans with just indignation.

4. In this state of things, Mr. Madison assembled Congress. They met in November, and on the 4th of June following (1812), declared war against England. This is called "*Madison's War*," because it was declared while he was President.

5. This declaration of war gave offence to many. They thought it unnecessary. They thought the difficulties might have been settled without resorting to arms. When my pupils are older, they can form an opinion for themselves.

6. It would make too large a volume to tell all about this war. On the *land*, the American army did not appear to much advantage. They attempted to take Canada, but failed to effect their object. On the *water*, the navy did much execution, and acquired signal honour.

7. The first naval battle was between the United States frigate *Constitution*, and the British frigate *Guerriere*. This was a dreadful engagement. The vessels were nearly equal, as to men and guns. Yet the British frigate was entirely dismasted, and otherwise so much injured, that she was set on fire by her conquerors, and consumed.

8. A second naval victory soon followed. This was the capture of the *Macedonian*, by the American frigate *United States*. The brave Commodore Decatur commanded the American frigate. In the action, the carpenter of the Macedonian was killed. He had

three little children, who were left to the care of their mother, who was a worthless woman. The *American* tars finding this out, gave the children 800 dollars from their wages. This was noble!

9. Next came the capture of the *Java* by the *Constitution*, and that of the *Peacock* by the *Hornet*. In this latter engagement, the Peacock struck in fifteen minutes. I am sorry to add, that so many balls had passed through her hull, that she sunk before all her men could be taken off.

10. You have heard, I presume, of the battle on *Lake Erie*. This was between two fleets. Commodore Perry commanded the American fleet, and after a desperate battle took the whole British fleet. He then sat down, and announced the victory in these words: "*We have met the enemy, and they are ours.*" This battle was fought Sept. 10, 1813.

11. The next year, 1814, August 23, six thousand British troops came up the Chesapeake, and took *Washington*, and burnt the capitol and the President's house. It was no credit to the Americans to suffer such an outrage, and was a disgrace to the British to be guilty of it.

12. On the 11th of September, was fought a celebrated naval battle, on Lake *Champlain*, between an American and British fleet. The British fleet consisted of seventeen vessels; that of the Americans of fourteen. The former had the advantage over the latter, both as to guns and men; yet the victory was so complete, that nearly the whole fleet fell into the hands of Commodore M'Donnough, the American Commander.

13. On the 24th of December, 1814, a *treaty of peace* was signed between the United States and England, which put an end to the war.

14. This treaty was signed at *Ghent*, in the Netherlands, at which place men from the United States and England met to settle all difficulties. Before the news arrived that peace had been agreed upon, the famous "*battle of New-Orleans*" took place. It was fought on the 8th of January, 1815. Gen. Jackson commanded the Americans, and obtained a splendid victory. In this battle, the British General Packenham was killed.

15. In 1817, Mr. Madison retired from office, and James Munroe was chosen President. Daniel D. Tompkins was chosen Vice-President.

QUESTIONS.

1. When did Mr. Madison become President? How long was he in office?
2. What is said of the difficulties which commenced while Mr. Jefferson was President? What of the attempts to settle them?
3. When were these difficulties increased? By what circumstance? What effect had this attack upon the American people?
4. What did Mr. Madison do? Where did Congress meet? When was war declared? What is this war called? Why?
5. What was thought of this war by many? Why?

6. In this war, how did the land forces appear? What did they attempt? Did the enterprise succeed? What is said of the naval force?
7. Between what vessels was the first engagement? Was it severe? Were the vessels nearly equal? Which gained the victory?
8. Between what vessels was the second engagement? Who commanded the American frigate? What story is told of the carpenter of the Macedonian?
9. What engagement next followed? What next? How soon did the Peacock strike? What is said of a part of her crew?
10. What engagement took place on Lake Erie? Who commanded the American fleet? Who conquered? What language did Commodore Perry use, when he announced the victory? When was this battle fought?
11. When did the British take Washington? What did they burn? What is said of this attack?
12. When did the engagement take place on Lake Champlain? Between what? How many vessels had the British? How many the Americans? Which had the advantage? Which conquered?
13. When was a treaty of peace signed?
14. Where was this treaty signed? Before the news arrived, what battle took place? Where? Who commanded the Americans? Who obtained the victory? What British General was killed?
15. When did Mr. Madison leave the Presidential chair? Who succeeded him? Who was chosen Vice-President?

STORY.

1. I might fill sheets with stories relating to the war, which I doubt not would greatly interest my readers. I could tell them of wonderful adventures—of hair-breadth escapes—of battles—of victories—of defeats. But I have room for but one story, and only a short one. The one I think of is affecting.

2. In Sept. 1814, a British squadron appeared off *Ston-*

ington, commanded by Sir Thomas Hardy. This is a small village, in the eastern part of Connecticut. Soon after the appearance of the squadron, a British boat was seen coming into the harbour. What could this mean?

3. In a few minutes a man landed from the boat, who bid the people remove the women and children, if they pleased, to a place of safety, for the town was soon to be laid in ashes.

4. Why such a cruel and unprovoked attack was made, I cannot say. What the people of Stonington had done to merit this, probably no one can tell. But an attack was made, and a dreadful one it was.

5. But the people were brave; and bravely did they defend themselves. In the course of the attack, several barges filled with British soldiers, attempted to land. Some of these barges were sunk. One drifted on shore, and in it was found a wounded midshipman.

6. It was a desperate wound which he had received; and it would not have been singular, had he been neglected. But no—although an enemy, he was kindly taken care of. He was young—handsome—brave—generous—a noble young man, though he was an enemy. Every one offered assistance—the old and the young seemed interested in him, and the physicians tried their utmost skill.

7. But it was all in vain. Death came, and he died With kindness was he buried, and with the honours of war; and many a tear was shed over one, who had thus fallen in a land of strangers.

8. Months rolled on. The war ended, and the events of the war were beginning to pass away; when one day, an elderly gentleman drove up to the village inn, and alighted.

9. He was evidently a foreigner, and a venerable man. "Sir," said he to the landlord, "during the late war this village, I think, suffered an attack."

10. 'It did,' replied the landlord. "Was there a British officer killed at that time?" inquired the stranger. 'There was one *wounded*, who afterwads died among us,' said the landlord. 'He was a youth in whom every one was interested, and could attention have saved him, he would not have died.'

11. The old man's eyes were lifted to Heaven! "Will you shew me where he lies?" inquired the stranger. The landlord now accompanied him to the spot, where he desired to be left alone.

12. Late at night, he returned to the inn, where he lodged. Early the following morning, he rose, and again repaired to the spot, where he spent several hours.

13. After a late breakfast, he called for his horse, and was about departing. 'Sir,' asked the landlord, may I venture to inquire whether the young midshipman was a relative of yours?'

14. "Yes, sir, he *was* a relative," replied the stranger. "He was a son—an only son—dearer to an old man's heart than all on earth besides. I have made this voyage with no other object than to find the spot where he was laid. I have found it—have seen it. I return contented. Thanks to God that he fell among a people who knew how to be generous even in war."

15. I doubt not my readers will feel sad, when they think of the sorrows which war often causes: but how delightful to see among enemies such instances of noble generosity and kindness, as that which we have here related!

General Washington crossing the Delaware. p. 136.

LESSON XXII.

JAMES MONROE, PRESIDENT.

1. On the 4th of March, 1817, Mr. Monroe was sworn into office, and continued in office for eight years.

2. The war having now ended, the condition of the country began to be more prosperous. Commerce revived in a measure ; and some manufacturing establishments were put in operation.

3. During the summer and autumn of this year, President Monroe made a *tour* through most of the states. The object of this tour was to gain information as to the state of the country, so that he might better administer the government. He was treated with great respect and attention in his tour.

4. During the session of Congress in 1817–18, a bill of much importance to the *indigent* officers and soldiers of the revolutionary army was passed. This provided to give twenty dollars per month to the former, and eight to the latter, during life. This was truly honourable to the United States; but no more than *just*, in view of the toils and privations of those who had fought for American liberty.

5. In 1818, the United States became involved in another war. This was with the *Seminole Indians.* These Indians lived partly in the United States, and partly in Florida.

The Indians were the aggressors. They committed several murders upon white people; and it became necessary to check them.

6. Gen. Jackson was appointed to superintend the war. In about a year, the Indians were subdued. But in conducting the war, Gen. Jackson was thought by many to have been unnecessarily severe. You can judge for yourselves, when you are older.

7. The remainder of Mr. Monroe's administration was not marked by any event of importance. The country continued to flourish. As a President, he was beloved and respected.

8. In 1825, he retired from office with the good wishes of his country, and was succeeded by John Quincy Adams. John C. Calhoun was chosen Vice-President.

QUESTIONS.

1. When did Mr. Monroe become President? How long did he continue in office?

2. What is said of the condition of the country after the war? What of commerce? What of manufacturing establishments?
3. What tour did Mr. Monroe make in 1817? What was the object of this tour? How was he treated?
4. What bill passed Congress in 1817–18? What did it provide? What is said of this measure?
5. What war took place in 1818? Where did these Indians live? Who were the aggresors? What did they do?
6. Who superintended the war? How long did it last? What did some think of Gen. Jackson's conduct in this war?
7. What is said of the remainder of Mr. Monroe's administration?
8. When did he retire from office? Who succeeded him as President? Who received the appointment of Vice-President?

STORY.

1. Soon after Mr. Monroe became President, he made the tour, as I told you, of most of the states. This was in 1817. Most of my pupils were either not then born, or were too young to know what took place, as he passed through the country.

2. It was a delightful spectacle to see the President of so large a country as the United States travel as Mr. Monroe did. In other countries, kings sometimes make a survey of their dominions. But *they* travel in great state—in a splendid coach—with horses loaded with gold or silver plate—with numerous servants richly dressed—and an armed band of soldiers to guard them. And then,

there is so much pride and pomp, as if they were a higher order of beings—made only to be *served*, and their subjects only to submit. No common man may speak to them: he may think himself honoured to be allowed to *look* at them.

3. But it was otherwise during the tour of Mr. Monroe. He travelled in a respectable style. This was proper. But his equipage was plain. He was a plain man, and kind and civil did he appear towards all who were pleased to call upon him. Men may be great, and yet free from odious pride. They may be high in office, and feel no disposition to trample others in the dust.

4. The modest appearance of Mr. Monroe justly pleased the people. *They* had elevated him to the high station which he occupied, and he was not disposed to despise them. Perceiving this, they paid him double honour. Citizens and soldiers—the old and the young—went forth to meet him as he approached; bells were rung—cannon were fired—processions were formed—entertainments were made. Even those who had voted for another man to be President, bid him welcome, and aided to make his journey pleasant.

5. What a peculiar, what a happy, country, my children, is ours! What simplicity of manners! what liberty is

enjoyed! what *equality* is preserved! Did you live in England, you could indulge no hope of being King of that country; nor could you be Emperor of Russia, were you there. But in the United States, the most ragged little boy that runs in the street may rise. Office is open to all who behave well. If you are a *boy*, *you* may be the *President* of the United States in some future time: if a *girl*, you may be a President's *wife*.

6. In travelling from Washington to New-York, Mr. Monroe passed through *Trenton*. This town lies in New-Jersey, on the east bank of the Delaware, 30 miles north-east from Philadelphia. This was an interesting spot to the President. Here was fought, Dec. 26, 1776, the celebrated battle of Trenton. At that time he was a lieutenant in the American army. There he fought, and was severely wounded.

7. Before this battle, the prospect of the Americans was quite gloomy. The American army had been compelled to retreat into Delaware. But, at length, Washington roused by the sad prospect before him, said something was to be done, or the country would be ruined. A body of British, it was told, were at Trenton. Washington collected his troops on the banks of the Delaware, an determined to pass that river, and, if possible, take them by surprise.

8. A writer says, "It was a dark, gloomy, and horrible night." A storm was raging. The hail rattled from above. The ice heaved, rolled, and tumbled, as the boats at *midnight* passed over the rapid current of the Delaware. But a propitious Providence smiled upon the attempt. The passage was made in safety. The British were taken by surprise; their commander was killed, and their army captured. This was an important victory for the Americans. It raised their desponding hopes; it roused them to higher action.

9. During the above contest, Mr. Monroe was wounded by a bullet, which passed through his shoulder. It proved not to be mortal, but was very severe; and long did he linger, and much did he suffer, before he recovered. Little did he *then* think, that forty years from that time he should visit the same spot, welcomed by thousands of freemen, and himself the President of a peaceful, wide-spread, and noble republic!

The cheated Indian. p. 143.

LESSON XXIII.

JOHN QUINCY ADAMS, PRESIDENT.

1. On the 4th of March, 1825, Mr. Adams took the usual oath to support the constitution, and became President of the United States. He held the office for four years.

2. At the time a new President was to be chosen, the people were much divided as to candidates. Some were for Mr. Adams; some

for General Jackson; others for Mr. Crawford; and others still for Mr. Clay. No choice being made by the people, it devolved on the House of Representatives in Congress to make the election.

3. It was an occasion of deep interest, when they met to decide. Each of the several parties in the United States were anxious to have their candidate succeed. At length, the votes were given in and counted. Mr. Adams had 87; Gen. Jackson 71; and Mr. Crawford 54. Mr. Adams having more than either of the others, was solemnly declared to be chosen.

4. As a President, Mr. Adams was not as popular as some who had preceded him. Yet the country continued to flourish while he was in office. Peace with other nations prevailed. The great debt contracted for the war was diminished. Numerous canals, rail-roads, and other public improvements, were begun.

5. During the years 1824 and 1825, the people of the United States were gratified with a visit from their old friend, Gen. La Fayette. At his own expense, he had come during the war of the revolution to aid them. He spent many thousands of dollars for us, and fought nobly for American Independence. During his visit, he was hailed as the friend and benefactor of America. It being understood that he was poor, Congress voted him two hundred thousand dollars, and a large tract of land. This was honourable to the nation ; yet it was due for what he had done and expended during the war. On the 7th of Sept. 1825, he sailed again for France. Congress despatched a new and beautiful frigate, called the Brandywine, to convey him home.

6. The year 1825 was distinguished for the completion of the great Erie Canal, in the state of New-York. This canal is 360 miles in

length. It connects Lake Erie with Hudson River at Albany. It was begun July 4th, 1817. The first boat from Lake Erie arrived at New-York Oct. 4th, 1825. The whole expense of the canal was more than nine millions of dollars.

7. On the 4th of July, 1826, occurred the deaths of the elder President Adams (the father of John Quincy Adams) and President Jefferson. This was just fifty years from the day Independence was declared. Both these great men assisted, in 1776, in framing the Declaration. It was wonderful that they should live 50 years from that date ; but more wonderful that both should die on the same day.

8. In 1829, there was a new election of President. The people were again much divided. The two candidates were Mr. Adams and Gen. Jackson. Each had powerful friends. Much was said and written for and against them by their respective parties. But when

the time arrived for the electors—that is, the persons appointed by the people to elect a President—to give their votes, it was found that Gen. Jackson had 178 votes, and Mr. Adams but 83.

9. Gen. Jackson being elected, was sworn into office on the 4th of March, 1829. He is now the President of the United States. Should he live, he will continue in office till 1832, when a new election will take place. Some think he will be elected again; others predict that Mr. Clay or Mr. Calhoun will be chosen. Time will tell.

QUESTIONS.

1. When did Mr. Adams enter upon the office of President? How long did he continue in office?

2. Were the people united in choosing Mr. Adams? Who besides him were candidates? Did the people make any choice? Who decided the question?

3. What is said of the occasion when the House of Representatives met to decide? How many votes had Mr. Adams? How many had Gen. Jackson? How many had Mr. Crawford? Who was therefore declared to be chosen?

4. Was Mr. Adams popular as a President? What is said of the country

during his administration? What of peace with other nations? What of the national debt? What of canals and rail-roads?

5. When did Gen. La Fayette visit the United States? What is said of him during the war of the revolution? How was he received during his visit? What did Congress do for him? What is said of this gift? When did he return home? In what way?

6. For what was the year 1825 distinguished? How long is the Erie Canal? What does it connect? When was it begun? When did the first boat from Lake Erie reach New-York? What was the expense of this canal?

7. What remarkable event took place July 4th, 1826? How long was this from the year Independence was declared?

8. In what year did a new election for President take place? Who were the candidates? What is meant by electors? Whom did the electors choose? How many votes had Gen. Jackson? How many had Mr. Adams?

9. When was Gen. Jackson sworn into office? When will his term of office expire? What is thought of his being re-elected? Who besides him are candidates?

STORY.

1. I have told you of the visit which La Fayette made to the people of the United States in 1825 and 1826. It would be pleasant to relate the wonderful adventures of his life. But I have not room for so long a story. I must content myself with telling an affecting incident, which took place while Fayette was passing through one of the western states.

2. Fayette and his company had stopped for the night in a small village, in which lived a white man, who was a

trader. Levasseur, the secretary of Fayette, entered the shop of the trader to purchase some articles. While standing near the counter, an Indian entered.

3. "Sir," said the Indian, "some whiskey!"—at the same time giving the trader a ninepence. The trader, taking the money, told the Indian to wait till he could help him. After some time, the Indian asked for his whiskey. 'You must pay for it, then,' said the trader. "I have given you ninepence already," said the Indian.

4. 'You scoundrel,' said the trader violently enraged, 'get out of my shop.' The Indian would have replied; but the trader sprung over the counter, darted upon the Indian, and brutally pushed him out of doors.

5. Levasseur was filled with indignation, but he had no time to interpose; indeed, as he was a stranger, prudence forbade him. He followed the Indian, however, out of doors. At a short distance from the shop, he found him standing like a marble statue. At length, crossing his arms upon his breast, the Indian directed his course towards a creek, which at no great distance crossed the road.

6. Levasseur followed. On the opposite side, the Indian paused—turned—clenched his hands—raised them—and at the same time directed his eyes towards Heaven,

and seemed to say, "Have the white people any God? will his vengeance sleep? will he never take pity on the poor Indians?"

7. Upon this, he again directed his course towards the forest, in the shades of which and the obscurity of night, he was soon lost.

8. 'Ah!' said Levasseur 'poor Indians! you are tempted by white men to purchase *poison*, and when you are willing to purchase it, you are cheated, robbed, beaten, and turned out of doors. White men call you savages; but are they not more savage than you?'

9. My pupils will allow me to give them a word of advice. You will soon become men. You will spread through the land. You may meet with the 'red men' of the forest. Treat them kindly, for they have souls as well as you. They were once owners of the land in which you dwell. They are dwindling away. Their bravest warriors are no more. Their boldest hunters are dead. The miserable remnants of their tribes should be fostered—taught the arts of civilized life—told of the Bible—of the Son of God—of Heaven, and how they may secure it. This may be done; but it must be done soon, or the only season will have for ever passed away.

www.ingramcontent.com/pod-product-compliance
Lightning Source LLC
Chambersburg PA
CBHW032229080426
42735CB00008B/771
* 9 7 8 1 4 7 3 3 2 4 7 7 0 *